250+ JAVA PROGRAMS WITH OUTPUT

BY ANIKET PATASKAR

PREFACE

Copyright © By Author
All rights reserved. No part of this book may be reproduced, stored in a retrieval system, or transmitted in any form or by any means, without the prior written permission of the author.
Every effort has been made in the preparation of this book to ensure the accuracy of the information presented. However, the information contained in this book is sold without warranty, either express or implied.
Neither the author, nor distributors will be held liable for any damages caused or alleged to be caused directly or indirectly by this book.

Author: Aniket Pataskar

Email: pataskaraniket@gmail.com

Contact: +91 9423448273

Cover Image by Aniket Pataskar

ABOUT THE AUTHOR

Aniket O. Pataskar is originally from India. He is IT software engineer with working experience on various programming languages.
250+ Java Programs With Output is a book with collection of programs for leaning. Aniket is always interested in emerging technologies of Apple.
Aniket has skills in Software development, IOS (iPhone & iPad) App Development as well as Android App Development & Multimedia such as - Animation, Image editing, Audio editing, Video editing & visual effects.

This book is dedicated to:

My family for their continued love and support, and for always believing in me. I also want to dedicate it to the god who always inspire me to do this.
This book would not have been possible without your love and under-standing.
Thank you from the bottom of my heart.

TABLE OF CONTENTS

1. Hello World 13
2. Sum of Two Numbers 14
3. Check Even or Odd 15
4. Print Numbers from 1 to 5 using Loop 16
5. Factorial of a Number 17
6. Reverse a String 18
7. Check if a Number is Prime 19
8. Find the Largest of Three Numbers 21
9. Simple Calculator 23
10. Fibonacci Series up to 10 Terms 24
11. Swapping Two Numbers 25
12. Sum of Digits of a Number 26
13. Reverse a Number 27
14. Palindrome Check for a Number 28
15. Calculate Power of a Number 30
16. Find the GCD of Two Numbers 31
17. Find LCM of Two Numbers 32
18. Check if a String is Palindrome 33
19. Count the Number of Digits in a Number 34
20. Convert Celsius to Fahrenheit 35
21. Convert Fahrenheit to Celsius 36
22. Find the Area of a Circle 37
23. Find the Perimeter of a Circle 38
24. Calculate Simple Interest 39
25. Calculate Compound Interest 40
26. Convert Decimal to Binary 41
27. Convert Binary to Decimal 42
28. Convert Decimal to Hexadecimal 43
29. Convert Hexadecimal to Decimal 44
30. Find ASCII Value of a Character 45
31. Find Sum of Natural Numbers 46
32. Find the Average of Numbers 47
33. Find the Smallest Number in an Array 48
34. Find the Largest Number in an Array 49
35. Find the Second Largest Number in an Array 50
36. Print a 2D Array 52
37. Transpose a Matrix 54
38. Find the Sum of Two Matrices 56
39. Find the Product of Two Matrices 58

40. Count the Number of Vowels in a String 61
41. Find the Frequency of Characters in a String 62
42. Remove Vowels from a String 64
43. Find the Length of a String 65
44. Check if a String Contains a Substring 66
45. Convert String to Uppercase 67
46. Convert String to Lowercase 68
47. Reverse a String 69
48. Find the Sum of Array Elements 70
49. Find the Average of Array Elements 71
50. Find the Minimum Element in an Array 72
51. Find the Maximum Element in an Array 73
52. Count the Occurrences of an Element in an Array 74
53. Check if an Array Contains a Given Element 75
54. Reverse an Array 76
55. Find the Second Largest Element in an Array 77
56. Find the Factorial of a Number Using Recursion ... 79
57. Find the Fibonacci Series Using Recursion 80
58. Find the Greatest Common Divisor Using Recursion 82
59. Find the Sum of Digits Using Recursion 83
60. Check if a String is a Palindrome Using Recursion 84
61. Find the Power of a Number Using Recursion 86
62. Convert Binary to Decimal 87
63. Convert Decimal to Binary 88
64. Convert Decimal to Hexadecimal 89
65. Convert Hexadecimal to Decimal 90
66. Swap Two Numbers Using a Temporary Variable 91
67. Swap Two Numbers Without Using a Temporary Variable 92
68. Reverse a Number 93
69. Check if a Number is an Armstrong Number 94
70. Check if a Number is a Prime Number 96
71. Find the LCM of Two Numbers 98
72. Find the HCF of Two Numbers 99
73. Check if a Number is Even or Odd 100
74. Generate a Random Number 101
75. Find the GCD of Two Numbers Using the Euclidean Algorithm 102
76. Find the Square Root of a Number 103

77. Check if a Number is a Perfect Square.................. 104
78. Check if a Number is a Palindrome 105
79. Find the Sum of Prime Numbers up to N 107
80. Find the Sum of Natural Numbers up to N 109
81. Convert a Character to its ASCII Value 110
82. Find the Sum of Even and Odd Numbers in an Array 111
83. Find the Product of Array Elements....................... 113
84. Find the Largest and Smallest Elements in an Array 114
85. Count the Number of Digits in a Number.............. 116
86. Print the Multiplication Table for a Number 117
87. Find the Sum of the Diagonals in a Matrix............ 119
88. Find the Transpose of a Matrix 121
89. Print the Fibonacci Series Without Recursion...... 123
90. Implement a Basic Calculator................................. 124
91. Check if Two Strings are Anagrams...................... 127
92. Find the Factorial of a Number Using Recursion. 129
93. Calculate the Power of a Number Using a Loop.. 130
94. Find the Sum of Natural Numbers Using Recursion.. 131
95. Find the Fibonacci Series Using Recursion 132
96. Calculate the Sum of Digits of a Number Using Recursion.. 134
97. Reverse a String Using Recursion......................... 135
98. Calculate the Greatest Common Divisor (GCD) Using Recursion.. 136
99. Print All Prime Numbers up to N Using a Method 137
100. Find the Length of a String Without Using length() Method.. 139
101. Find the First Non-Repeated Character in a String 140
102. Check if a Number is a Palindrome Using Recursion.. 142
103. Count the Number of Words in a String.............. 144
104. Find the Second Largest Number in an Array.... 145
105. Calculate the Sum of All Prime Numbers in an Array 147
106. Replace All Vowels in a String with a Specific Character 149
107. Find the Largest Palindrome in an Array 150

108. Count the Number of Vowels and Consonants in a String 152
109. Check if a Number is an Armstrong Number 154
110. Convert a Decimal Number to Binary.................. 156
111. Convert a Binary Number to Decimal.................. 157
112. Convert a Decimal Number to Hexadecimal 158
113. Convert a Hexadecimal Number to Decimal 159
114. Find the HCF and LCM of Two Numbers 160
115. Reverse a Number Using Recursion................... 161
116. Find the Sum of Even Numbers in an Array....... 162
117. Check if a String is a Palindrome Using a Loop 163
118. Find the Number of Digits in an Integer 165
119. Generate a Multiplication Table for a Given Number.. 166
120. Calculate the Area of a Rectangle....................... 168
121. Check if a Number is Even or Odd 169
122. Find the Smallest Number in an Array 170
123. Convert Celsius to Fahrenheit............................. 171
124. Find the Sum of Odd Numbers in an Array 172
125. Check if a Year is a Leap Year 173
126. Calculate the Area of a Circle 174
127. Calculate the Area of a Triangle 175
128. Find the GCD of Two Numbers Using a Loop ... 176
129. Calculate the LCM of Two Numbers Using a Loop... 177
130. Find the Maximum and Minimum Values in an Array 178
131. Calculate the Perimeter of a Rectangle.............. 180
132. Swap Two Numbers Without Using a Temporary Variable 181
133. Find the Second Smallest Number in an Array.. 182
134. Find the Length of a String 183
135. Count the Number of Words in a String.............. 184
136. Calculate the Square Root of a Number............. 185
137. Convert a String to Uppercase............................ 186
138. Convert a String to Lowercase............................ 187
139. Reverse a String Using a Loop 188
140. Calculate the Factorial of a Number Using Recursion.. 189
141. Count the Frequency of Each Character in a String 190

142. Find the First Non-Repeated Character in a String 192
143. Generate Fibonacci Series up to N Terms 194
144. Find the Nth Fibonacci Number Using Recursion 196
145. Remove Duplicates from an Array 197
146. Check if Two Strings are Anagrams 198
147. Reverse the Words in a Sentence 200
148. Check if a String is a Substring of Another String 201
149. Find the Sum of the Diagonal Elements in a Matrix 202
150. Find the Sum of Each Row in a Matrix 203
151. Find the Sum of Each Column in a Matrix 205
152. Check if a Matrix is Symmetric 207
153. Find the Trace of a Matrix 209
154. Rotate a Matrix 90 Degrees Clockwise 210
155. Print a Pascal's Triangle 212
156. Find the GCD (Greatest Common Divisor) of Two Numbers Using Euclidean Algorithm 214
157. Implement Bubble Sort Algorithm 215
158. Implement Selection Sort Algorithm 217
159. Implement Insertion Sort Algorithm 219
160. Implement Merge Sort Algorithm 221
161. Implement Quick Sort Algorithm 225
162. Implement Binary Search Algorithm 228
163. Check if an Array is Sorted in Ascending Order 231
164. Find the Median of an Array 233
165. Count the Number of Vowels and Consonants in a String 235
166. Convert a Decimal Number to Binary 237
167. Convert a Binary Number to Decimal 238
168. Check if a Number is Palindrome 239
169. Check if a String is Palindrome 241
170. Find the Largest Element in an Array 242
171. Find the Smallest Element in an Array 243
172. Reverse an Array 244
173. Sum of Diagonals in a Matrix 245
174. Find the Second Largest Element in an Array ... 247
175. Find the Frequency of Each Element in an Array 249

176. Convert a String to Uppercase Without Using Built-In Function 250
177. Convert a String to Lowercase Without Using Built-In Function 251
178. Find the Maximum and Minimum Elements in an Array 252
179. Check if Two Strings are Anagrams.................... 254
180. Calculate the Power of a Number........................ 256
181. Implement a Simple Calculator 257
182. Print Fibonacci Series Up to N Terms................. 260
183. Count the Number of Words in a String............. 261
184. Find the Sum of All Odd Numbers from 1 to N .. 262
185. Find the Sum of All Even Numbers from 1 to N. 263
186. Count the Number of Vowels in a String 264
187. Generate a Random Number Between 1 and 100 265
188. Count the Number of Digits in an Integer 266
189. Print a Right-Angle Triangle Pattern.................... 267
190. Print a Pyramid Pattern 269
191. Print a Diamond Pattern.. 271
192. Print the Multiplication Table of a Given Number.. 274
193. Check if a Number is Prime.................................. 276
194. Calculate Factorial of a Number 278
195. Find the Sum of Natural Numbers up to N 279
196. Print the Fibonacci Series Using Recursion....... 280
197. Find the Sum of Digits of a Number 281
198. Check if a Number is Even or Odd...................... 282
199. Count the Number of Spaces in a String 283
200. Find the Common Elements Between Two Arrays 284
201. Convert Binary to Decimal 286
202. Convert Decimal to Binary 287
203. Swap Two Numbers Without Using a Temporary Variable 288
204. Check if a Number is Armstrong.......................... 289
205. Check if a Number is Perfect................................ 291
206. Check if a String is a Palindrome (Ignoring Case)... 293
207. Find the Sum of All Prime Numbers up to N 294
208. Find the GCD of Two Numbers............................ 296

209. Find the LCM of Two Numbers 297
210. Convert Celsius to Fahrenheit............................. 298
211. Convert Fahrenheit to Celsius............................. 299
212. Count the Number of Consonants in a String 300
213. Find the Factorial of a Number Using Recursion.. 301
214. Reverse a Number... 302
215. Find the First Non-Repeated Character in a String 303
216. Print the Fibonacci Series Using a While Loop.. 305
217. Generate the First N Prime Numbers................. 307
218. Find the Largest Element in an Array................. 309
219. Find the Smallest Element in an Array............... 310
220. Check if Two Strings Are Anagrams 311
221. Calculate the Power of a Number Using a Loop 313
222. Find the Second Largest Element in an Array ... 314
223. Find the Second Smallest Element in an Array . 316
224. Calculate the Average of Elements in an Array . 318
225. Find the Maximum and Minimum Values in an Array 319
226. Find the Sum of Each Row in a 2D Array........... 321
227. Find the Sum of Each Column in a 2D Array 323
228. Reverse the Elements of an Array....................... 325
229. Merge Two Arrays into a Single Array 326
230. Rotate an Array to the Left by One Position....... 327
231. Rotate an Array to the Right by One Position 328
232. Count the Number of Words in a String.............. 329
233. Convert a Character to its ASCII Value 330
234. Find the Length of a String Without Using length() Method.. 331
235. Find the Sum of the Elements in a 2D Array...... 332
236. Transpose a 2D Matrix.. 334
237. Multiply Two Matrices.. 337
238. Count the Number of Vowels in a String 339
239. Count the Number of Consonants in a String 340
240. Find the Sum of Even and Odd Numbers in an Array Separately 341
241. Find the Factorial of a Number Using Recursion.. 343
242. Find the Greatest Common Divisor (GCD) Using Recursion.. 344

243. Find the Least Common Multiple (LCM) Using GCD 345
244. Calculate the Power of a Number Using Recursion 346
245. Print Fibonacci Series Using Recursion 348
246. Reverse a String Using Recursion 350
247. Check if a String is a Palindrome Using Recursion 351
248. Check if a Number is Prime 353
249. Find the First N Prime Numbers 355
250. Find the Nth Fibonacci Number 357
251. Convert Decimal to Binary 358
252. Convert Binary to Decimal 359
253. Find the Largest Element in a 2D Array 360
254. Check if a Number is Armstrong 362
255. Find the Sum of Digits of a Number 364
256. Reverse a Number 365
257. Check if a Number is Palindrome 366
258. Find the Frequency of Each Character in a String 368

1. HELLO WORLD

```java
public class HelloWorld {
    public static void main(String[] args) {
        System.out.println("Hello, World!");
    }
}
```

Output:

Hello, World!

2. SUM OF TWO NUMBERS

```java
public class SumOfTwoNumbers {
    public static void main(String[] args) {
        int num1 = 10;
        int num2 = 20;
        int sum = num1 + num2;
        System.out.println("Sum: " + sum);
    }
}
```

Output:

Sum: 30

3. CHECK EVEN OR ODD

```java
public class EvenOdd {
    public static void main(String[] args) {
        int num = 7;
        if (num % 2 == 0) {
            System.out.println(num + " is even.");
        } else {
            System.out.println(num + " is odd.");
        }
    }
}
```

Output:

7 is odd.

4. PRINT NUMBERS FROM 1 TO 5 USING LOOP

```java
public class PrintNumbers {
    public static void main(String[] args) {
        for (int i = 1; i <= 5; i++) {
            System.out.println(i);
        }
    }
}
```

Output:

1

2

3

4

5

5. FACTORIAL OF A NUMBER

```java
public class Factorial {
    public static void main(String[] args) {
        int num = 5;
        int factorial = 1;
        for (int i = 1; i <= num; i++) {
            factorial *= i;
        }
        System.out.println("Factorial of " + num + " is " + factorial);
    }
}
```

Output:

Factorial of 5 is 120

6. REVERSE A STRING

```java
public class ReverseString {
    public static void main(String[] args) {
        String str = "Java";
        String reversed = new StringBuilder(str).reverse().toString();
        System.out.println("Reversed String: " + reversed);
    }
}
```

Output:

Reversed String: avaJ

7. CHECK IF A NUMBER IS PRIME

```java
public class PrimeNumber {
    public static void main(String[] args) {
        int num = 29;
        boolean isPrime = true;
        for (int i = 2; i <= num / 2; i++) {
            if (num % i == 0) {
                isPrime = false;
                break;
            }
        }
        if (isPrime) {
            System.out.println(num + " is a prime number.");
        } else {
            System.out.println(num + " is not a prime number.");
        }
```

        }
}

Output:

29 is a prime number.

8. FIND THE LARGEST OF THREE NUMBERS

```java
public class LargestNumber {
    public static void main(String[] args) {
        int num1 = 25, num2 = 78, num3 = 87;
        int largest;
        if (num1 >= num2 && num1 >= num3) {
            largest = num1;
        } else if (num2 >= num1 && num2 >= num3) {
            largest = num2;
        } else {
            largest = num3;
        }
        System.out.println("Largest number is: " + largest);
    }
```

}

Output:

Largest number is: 87

9. SIMPLE CALCULATOR

```java
public class SimpleCalculator {
    public static void main(String[] args) {
        int num1 = 10, num2 = 5;
        System.out.println("Addition: " + (num1 + num2));
        System.out.println("Subtraction: " + (num1 - num2));
        System.out.println("Multiplication: " + (num1 * num2));
        System.out.println("Division: " + (num1 / num2));
    }
}
```

Output:

Addition: 15

Subtraction: 5

Multiplication: 50

Division: 2

10. FIBONACCI SERIES UP TO 10 TERMS

```java
public class FibonacciSeries {
    public static void main(String[] args) {
        int num1 = 0, num2 = 1;
        System.out.print("Fibonacci Series: " + num1 + ", " + num2);
        for (int i = 3; i <= 10; i++) {
            int next = num1 + num2;
            System.out.print(", " + next);
            num1 = num2;
            num2 = next;
        }
    }
}
```

Output:

Fibonacci Series: 0, 1, 1, 2, 3, 5, 8, 13, 21, 34

11. SWAPPING TWO NUMBERS

```java
public class SwapNumbers {
    public static void main(String[] args) {
        int a = 5, b = 10;
        System.out.println("Before Swap: a = " + a + ", b = " + b);
        int temp = a;
        a = b;
        b = temp;
        System.out.println("After Swap: a = " + a + ", b = " + b);
    }
}
```

Output:

Before Swap: a = 5, b = 10

After Swap: a = 10, b = 5

12. SUM OF DIGITS OF A NUMBER

```java
public class SumOfDigits {
    public static void main(String[] args) {
        int num = 1234;
        int sum = 0;
        while (num != 0) {
            sum += num % 10;
            num /= 10;
        }
        System.out.println("Sum of digits: " + sum);
    }
}
```

Output:

Sum of digits: 10

13. REVERSE A NUMBER

```java
public class ReverseNumber {
    public static void main(String[] args) {
        int num = 1234;
        int reversed = 0;
        while (num != 0) {
            int digit = num % 10;
            reversed = reversed * 10 + digit;
            num /= 10;
        }
        System.out.println("Reversed Number: " + reversed);
    }
}
```

Output:

Reversed Number: 4321

14. PALINDROME CHECK FOR A NUMBER

```java
public class PalindromeNumber {
    public static void main(String[] args) {
        int num = 121, originalNum = num, reversed = 0;
        while (num != 0) {
            int digit = num % 10;
            reversed = reversed * 10 + digit;
            num /= 10;
        }
        if (originalNum == reversed) {
            System.out.println(originalNum + " is a palindrome.");
        } else {
            System.out.println(originalNum + " is not a palindrome.");
        }
    }
}
```

}

Output:

121 is a palindrome.

15. CALCULATE POWER OF A NUMBER

```java
public class PowerOfNumber {
    public static void main(String[] args) {
        int base = 2, exponent = 3;
        int result = 1;
        for (int i = 0; i < exponent; i++) {
            result *= base;
        }
        System.out.println(base + " to the power of " + exponent + " is " + result);
    }
}
```

Output:

2 to the power of 3 is 8

16. FIND THE GCD OF TWO NUMBERS

```java
public class GCD {
    public static void main(String[] args) {
        int num1 = 54, num2 = 24;
        while (num1 != num2) {
            if (num1 > num2) {
                num1 -= num2;
            } else {
                num2 -= num1;
            }
        }
        System.out.println("GCD is: " + num1);
    }
}
```

Output:

GCD is: 6

17. FIND LCM OF TWO NUMBERS

```java
public class LCM {
    public static void main(String[] args) {
        int num1 = 4, num2 = 6, lcm;
        lcm = (num1 > num2) ? num1 : num2;
        while (true) {
            if (lcm % num1 == 0 && lcm % num2 == 0) {
                System.out.println("LCM is: " + lcm);
                break;
            }
            lcm++;
        }
    }
}
```

Output:

LCM is: 12

18. CHECK IF A STRING IS PALINDROME

```java
public class PalindromeString {
    public static void main(String[] args) {
        String str = "radar";
        String reversed = new StringBuilder(str).reverse().toString();
        if (str.equals(reversed)) {
            System.out.println(str + " is a palindrome.");
        } else {
            System.out.println(str + " is not a palindrome.");
        }
    }
}
```

Output:

radar is a palindrome.

19. COUNT THE NUMBER OF DIGITS IN A NUMBER

```java
public class CountDigits {
    public static void main(String[] args) {
        int num = 12345;
        int count = 0;
        while (num != 0) {
            num /= 10;
            count++;
        }
        System.out.println("Number of digits: " + count);
    }
}
```

Output:

Number of digits: 5

20. CONVERT CELSIUS TO FAHRENHEIT

```java
public class CelsiusToFahrenheit {
    public static void main(String[] args) {
        double celsius = 25;
        double fahrenheit = (celsius * 9/5) + 32;
        System.out.println(celsius + " °C = " + fahrenheit + " °F");
    }
}
```

Output:

25.0 °C = 77.0 °F

21. CONVERT FAHRENHEIT TO CELSIUS

```java
public class FahrenheitToCelsius {
    public static void main(String[] args) {
        double fahrenheit = 77;
        double celsius = (fahrenheit - 32) * 5/9;
        System.out.println(fahrenheit + " °F = " + celsius + " °C");
    }
}
```

Output:

77.0 °F = 25.0 °C

22. FIND THE AREA OF A CIRCLE

```java
public class AreaOfCircle {
    public static void main(String[] args) {
        double radius = 7.5;
        double area = Math.PI * radius * radius;
        System.out.println("Area of the circle: " + area);
    }
}
```

Output:

Area of the circle: 176.71458676442586

23. FIND THE PERIMETER OF A CIRCLE

```java
public class PerimeterOfCircle {
    public static void main(String[] args) {
        double radius = 7.5;
        double perimeter = 2 * Math.PI * radius;
        System.out.println("Perimeter of the circle: " + perimeter);
    }
}
```

Output:

Perimeter of the circle: 47.12388980384689

24. CALCULATE SIMPLE INTEREST

```java
public class SimpleInterest {
    public static void main(String[] args) {
        double principal = 1000, rate = 5, time = 2;
        double interest = (principal * rate * time) / 100;
        System.out.println("Simple Interest: " + interest);
    }
}
```

Output:

Simple Interest: 100.0

25. CALCULATE COMPOUND INTEREST

```java
public class CompoundInterest {
    public static void main(String[] args) {
        double principal = 1000, rate = 5, time = 2, compoundInterest;
        compoundInterest = principal * Math.pow((1 + rate / 100), time) - principal;
        System.out.println("Compound Interest: " + compoundInterest);
    }
}
```

Output:

Compound Interest: 102.5

26. CONVERT DECIMAL TO BINARY

```java
public class DecimalToBinary {
    public static void main(String[] args) {
        int decimal = 10;
        String binary = Integer.toBinaryString(decimal);
        System.out.println("Binary of " + decimal + " is: " + binary);
    }
}
```

Output:

Binary of 10 is: 1010

27. CONVERT BINARY TO DECIMAL

```java
public class BinaryToDecimal {
    public static void main(String[] args) {
        String binary = "1010";
        int decimal = Integer.parseInt(binary, 2);
        System.out.println("Decimal of " + binary + " is: " + decimal);
    }
}
```

Output:

Decimal of 1010 is: 10

28. CONVERT DECIMAL TO HEXADECIMAL

```java
public class DecimalToHexadecimal {
    public static void main(String[] args) {
        int decimal = 255;
        String hex = Integer.toHexString(decimal);
        System.out.println("Hexadecimal of " + decimal + " is: " + hex);
    }
}
```

Output:

Hexadecimal of 255 is: ff

29. CONVERT HEXADECIMAL TO DECIMAL

```java
public class HexadecimalToDecimal {
    public static void main(String[] args) {
        String hex = "ff";
        int decimal = Integer.parseInt(hex, 16);
        System.out.println("Decimal of " + hex + " is: " + decimal);
    }
}
```

Output:

Decimal of ff is: 255

30. FIND ASCII VALUE OF A CHARACTER

```java
public class ASCIIValue {
    public static void main(String[] args) {
        char ch = 'A';
        int asciiValue = ch;
        System.out.println("ASCII value of " + ch + " is: " + asciiValue);
    }
}
```

Output:

ASCII value of A is: 65

31. FIND SUM OF NATURAL NUMBERS

```java
public class SumOfNaturalNumbers {
    public static void main(String[] args) {
        int num = 10, sum = 0;
        for (int i = 1; i <= num; ++i) {
            sum += i;
        }
        System.out.println("Sum of natural numbers up to " + num + " is: " + sum);
    }
}
```

Output:

Sum of natural numbers up to 10 is: 55

32. FIND THE AVERAGE OF NUMBERS

```java
public class AverageOfNumbers {
    public static void main(String[] args) {
        int[] numbers = {2, 3, 5, 7, 11};
        double sum = 0;
        for (int num : numbers) {
            sum += num;
        }
        double average = sum / numbers.length;
        System.out.println("Average: " + average);
    }
}
```

Output:

Average: 5.6

33. FIND THE SMALLEST NUMBER IN AN ARRAY

```java
public class SmallestNumber {
    public static void main(String[] args) {
        int[] numbers = {3, 5, 2, 8, 1};
        int smallest = numbers[0];
        for (int num : numbers) {
            if (num < smallest) {
                smallest = num;
            }
        }
        System.out.println("Smallest number: " + smallest);
    }
}
```

Output:

Smallest number: 1

34. FIND THE LARGEST NUMBER IN AN ARRAY

```java
public class LargestNumberArray {
    public static void main(String[] args) {
        int[] numbers = {3, 5, 2, 8, 1};
        int largest = numbers[0];
        for (int num : numbers) {
            if (num > largest) {
                largest = num;
            }
        }
        System.out.println("Largest number: " + largest);
    }
}
```

Output:

Largest number: 8

35. FIND THE SECOND LARGEST NUMBER IN AN ARRAY

```java
public class SecondLargest {
    public static void main(String[] args) {
        int[] numbers = {3, 5, 2, 8, 1};
        int firstLargest, secondLargest;
        firstLargest = secondLargest = Integer.MIN_VALUE;
        for (int num : numbers) {
            if (num > firstLargest) {
                secondLargest = firstLargest;
                firstLargest = num;
            } else if (num > secondLargest && num != firstLargest) {
                secondLargest = num;
            }
        }
        System.out.println("Second largest number: " + secondLargest);
```

    }
}

Output:

Second largest number: 5

36. PRINT A 2D ARRAY

```java
public class Print2DArray {
    public static void main(String[] args) {
        int[][] array = {
            {1, 2, 3},
            {4, 5, 6},
            {7, 8, 9}
        };
        for (int i = 0; i < array.length; i++) {
            for (int j = 0; j < array[i].length; j++) {
                System.out.print(array[i][j] + " ");
            }
            System.out.println();
        }
    }
}
```

Output:

1 2 3
4 5 6
7 8 9

37. TRANSPOSE A MATRIX

```java
public class TransposeMatrix {
    public static void main(String[] args) {
        int[][] matrix = {
            {1, 2, 3},
            {4, 5, 6},
            {7, 8, 9}
        };
        int[][] transpose = new int[matrix[0].length][matrix.length];
        for (int i = 0; i < matrix.length; i++) {
            for (int j = 0; j < matrix[i].length; j++) {
                transpose[j][i] = matrix[i][j];
            }
        }
        for (int i = 0; i < transpose.length; i++) {
```

```java
        for (int j = 0; j < transpose[i].length; j++) {
            System.out.print(transpose[i][j] + " ");
        }
        System.out.println();
    }
  }
}
```

Output:

Copy code

1 4 7

2 5 8

3 6 9

38. FIND THE SUM OF TWO MATRICES

```java
public class MatrixAddition {
    public static void main(String[] args) {
        int[][] matrix1 = {
            {1, 2, 3},
            {4, 5, 6},
            {7, 8, 9}
        };
        int[][] matrix2 = {
            {9, 8, 7},
            {6, 5, 4},
            {3, 2, 1}
        };
        int[][] sum = new int[3][3];
        for (int i = 0; i < matrix1.length; i++) {
            for (int j = 0; j < matrix1[i].length; j++) {
```

```java
            sum[i][j] = matrix1[i][j] + matrix2[i][j];
        }
    }
    for (int i = 0; i < sum.length; i++) {
        for (int j = 0; j < sum[i].length; j++) {
            System.out.print(sum[i][j] + " ");
        }
        System.out.println();
    }
  }
}
```

Output:

10 10 10

10 10 10

10 10 10

39. FIND THE PRODUCT OF TWO MATRICES

```java
public class MatrixMultiplication {
    public static void main(String[] args) {
        int[][] matrix1 = {
            {1, 2, 3},
            {4, 5, 6},
            {7, 8, 9}
        };
        int[][] matrix2 = {
            {9, 8, 7},
            {6, 5, 4},
            {3, 2, 1}
        };
        int[][] product = new int[3][3];
        for (int i = 0; i < matrix1.length; i++) {
            for (int j = 0; j < matrix2[0].length; j++) {
```

```java
            for (int k = 0; k < matrix1[0].length; k++) {
                product[i][j] += matrix1[i][k] * matrix2[k][j];
            }
        }
    }
    for (int i = 0; i < product.length; i++) {
        for (int j = 0; j < product[i].length; j++) {
            System.out.print(product[i][j] + " ");
        }
        System.out.println();
    }
  }
}
```

Output:

30 24 18

84 69 54

138 114 90

40. COUNT THE NUMBER OF VOWELS IN A STRING

```java
public class CountVowels {
    public static void main(String[] args) {
        String str = "Hello World";
        int count = 0;
        for (int i = 0; i < str.length(); i++) {
            char ch = str.charAt(i);
            if (ch == 'a' || ch == 'e' || ch == 'i' || ch == 'o' || ch == 'u' ||
                ch == 'A' || ch == 'E' || ch == 'I' || ch == 'O' || ch == 'U') {
                count++; }
        }
        System.out.println("Number of vowels: " + count);
    }
}
```

Output:

Number of vowels: 3

41. FIND THE FREQUENCY OF CHARACTERS IN A STRING

```java
import java.util.HashMap;
import java.util.Map;

public class FrequencyOfCharacters {
    public static void main(String[] args) {
        String str = "Hello World";
        Map<Character, Integer> frequencyMap = new HashMap<>();
        for (int i = 0; i < str.length(); i++) {
            char ch = str.charAt(i);
            frequencyMap.put(ch, frequencyMap.getOrDefault(ch, 0) + 1);
        }
        for (Map.Entry<Character, Integer> entry : frequencyMap.entrySet()) {
            System.out.println(entry.getKey() + ": " + entry.getValue());
        }
```

    }
}

Output:

makefile

Copy code

H: 1

e: 1

l: 3

o: 2

 : 1

W: 1

r: 1

d: 1

42. REMOVE VOWELS FROM A STRING

```java
public class RemoveVowels {
    public static void main(String[] args) {
        String str = "Hello World";
        String result = str.replaceAll("[aeiouAEIOU]", "");
        System.out.println("String without vowels: " + result);
    }
}
```

Output:

String without vowels: Hll Wrld

43. FIND THE LENGTH OF A STRING

```java
public class StringLength {
    public static void main(String[] args) {
        String str = "Hello World";
        int length = str.length();
        System.out.println("Length of the string: " + length);
    }
}
```

Output:

Length of the string: 11

44. CHECK IF A STRING CONTAINS A SUBSTRING

```java
public class ContainsSubstring {
    public static void main(String[] args) {
        String str = "Hello World";
        String substring = "World";
        boolean contains = str.contains(substring);
        System.out.println("Contains '" + substring + "': " + contains);
    }
}
```

Output:

Contains 'World': true

45. CONVERT STRING TO UPPERCASE

```java
public class ConvertToUppercase {
    public static void main(String[] args) {
        String str = "hello world";
        String uppercaseStr = str.toUpperCase();
        System.out.println("Uppercase: " + uppercaseStr);
    }
}
```

Output:

Uppercase: HELLO WORLD

46. CONVERT STRING TO LOWERCASE

```java
public class ConvertToLowercase {
    public static void main(String[] args) {
        String str = "HELLO WORLD";
        String lowercaseStr = str.toLowerCase();
        System.out.println("Lowercase: " + lowercaseStr);
    }
}
```

Output:

Lowercase: hello world

47. REVERSE A STRING

```java
public class ReverseString {
    public static void main(String[] args) {
        String str = "Hello World";
        String reversed = new StringBuilder(str).reverse().toString();
        System.out.println("Reversed string: " + reversed);
    }
}
```

Output:

Reversed string: dlroW olleH

48. FIND THE SUM OF ARRAY ELEMENTS

```java
public class SumOfArray {
    public static void main(String[] args) {
        int[] array = {1, 2, 3, 4, 5};
        int sum = 0;
        for (int num : array) {
            sum += num;
        }
        System.out.println("Sum of array elements: " + sum);
    }
}
```

Output:

Sum of array elements: 15

49. FIND THE AVERAGE OF ARRAY ELEMENTS

```java
public class AverageOfArray {
    public static void main(String[] args) {
        int[] array = {1, 2, 3, 4, 5};
        double sum = 0;
        for (int num : array) {
            sum += num;
        }
        double average = sum / array.length;
        System.out.println("Average of array elements: " + average);
    }
}
```

Output:

Average of array elements: 3.0

50. FIND THE MINIMUM ELEMENT IN AN ARRAY

```java
public class MinimumElementArray {
    public static void main(String[] args) {
        int[] array = {1, 2, 3, 4, 5};
        int min = array[0];
        for (int num : array) {
            if (num < min) {
                min = num;
            }
        }
        System.out.println("Minimum element in array: " + min);
    }
}
```

Output:

Minimum element in array: 1

51. FIND THE MAXIMUM ELEMENT IN AN ARRAY

```java
public class MaximumElementArray {
    public static void main(String[] args) {
        int[] array = {1, 2, 3, 4, 5};
        int max = array[0];
        for (int num : array) {
            if (num > max) {
                max = num;
            }
        }
        System.out.println("Maximum element in array: " + max);
    }
}
```

Output:

Maximum element in array: 5

52. COUNT THE OCCURRENCES OF AN ELEMENT IN AN ARRAY

```java
public class CountOccurrences {
    public static void main(String[] args) {
        int[] array = {1, 2, 3, 2, 4, 2, 5};
        int target = 2;
        int count = 0;
        for (int num : array) {
            if (num == target) {
                count++;
            }
        }
        System.out.println("Occurrences of " + target + ": " + count);
    }
}
```

Output:

Occurrences of 2: 3

53. CHECK IF AN ARRAY CONTAINS A GIVEN ELEMENT

```java
public class ContainsElementArray {
    public static void main(String[] args) {
        int[] array = {1, 2, 3, 4, 5};
        int target = 3;
        boolean found = false;
        for (int num : array) {
            if (num == target) {
                found = true;
                break;
            }
        }
        System.out.println("Array contains " + target + ": " + found);
    }
}
```

Output:

Array contains 3: true

54. REVERSE AN ARRAY

```java
public class ReverseArray {
    public static void main(String[] args) {
        int[] array = {1, 2, 3, 4, 5};
        for (int i = 0, j = array.length - 1; i < j; i++, j--) {
            int temp = array[i];
            array[i] = array[j];
            array[j] = temp;
        }
        System.out.print("Reversed array: ");
        for (int num : array) {
            System.out.print(num + " ");
        }
    }
}
```

Output:

Reversed array: 5 4 3 2 1

55. FIND THE SECOND LARGEST ELEMENT IN AN ARRAY

```java
public class SecondLargestArray {

    public static void main(String[] args) {

        int[] array = {1, 2, 3, 4, 5};

        int firstLargest = Integer.MIN_VALUE;

        int secondLargest = Integer.MIN_VALUE;

        for (int num : array) {

            if (num > firstLargest) {

                secondLargest = firstLargest;

                firstLargest = num;

            } else if (num > secondLargest && num != firstLargest) {

                secondLargest = num;

            }

        }
```

```java
        System.out.println("Second largest element: " + secondLargest);
    }
}
```

Output:

Second largest element: 4

56. FIND THE FACTORIAL OF A NUMBER USING RECURSION

```java
public class FactorialRecursion {
    public static void main(String[] args) {
        int num = 5;
        int factorial = factorial(num);
        System.out.println("Factorial of " + num + " is: " + factorial);
    }


    public static int factorial(int num) {
        if (num == 0) {
            return 1;
        }
        return num * factorial(num - 1);
    }
}
```

Output:

Factorial of 5 is: 120

57. FIND THE FIBONACCI SERIES USING RECURSION

```java
public class FibonacciRecursion {
    public static void main(String[] args) {
        int count = 10;
        for (int i = 0; i < count; i++) {
            System.out.print(fibonacci(i) + " ");
        }
    }


    public static int fibonacci(int num) {
        if (num <= 1) {
            return num;
        }
        return fibonacci(num - 1) + fibonacci(num - 2);
    }
}
```

Output:

0 1 1 2 3 5 8 13 21 34

58. FIND THE GREATEST COMMON DIVISOR USING RECURSION

```java
public class GCDRecursion {
    public static void main(String[] args) {
        int num1 = 54, num2 = 24;
        int gcd = gcd(num1, num2);
        System.out.println("GCD is: " + gcd);
    }


    public static int gcd(int num1, int num2) {
        if (num2 == 0) {
            return num1;
        }
        return gcd(num2, num1 % num2);
    }
}
```

Output:

GCD is: 6

59. FIND THE SUM OF DIGITS USING RECURSION

```java
public class SumOfDigitsRecursion {
    public static void main(String[] args) {
        int num = 1234;
        int sum = sumOfDigits(num);
        System.out.println("Sum of digits: " + sum);
    }
    public static int sumOfDigits(int num) {
        if (num == 0) {
            return 0;
        }
        return num % 10 + sumOfDigits(num / 10);
    }
}
```

Output:

Sum of digits: 10

60. CHECK IF A STRING IS A PALINDROME USING RECURSION

```java
public class PalindromeRecursion {
    public static void main(String[] args) {
        String str = "madam";
        boolean isPalindrome = isPalindrome(str, 0, str.length() - 1);
        System.out.println("Is palindrome: " + isPalindrome);
    }


    public static boolean isPalindrome(String str, int start, int end) {
        if (start >= end) {
            return true;
        }
        if (str.charAt(start) != str.charAt(end)) {
            return false;
```

```
        }
        return isPalindrome(str, start + 1, end - 1);
    }
}
```

Output:

Is palindrome: true

61. FIND THE POWER OF A NUMBER USING RECURSION

```java
public class PowerRecursion {
    public static void main(String[] args) {
        int base = 2, exponent = 3;
        int result = power(base, exponent);
        System.out.println(base + "^" + exponent + " = " + result);
    }
    public static int power(int base, int exponent) {
        if (exponent == 0) {
            return 1;
        }
        return base * power(base, exponent - 1);
    }
}
```

Output:

2^3 = 8

62. CONVERT BINARY TO DECIMAL

```java
public class BinaryToDecimal {
    public static void main(String[] args) {
        String binary = "1010";
        int decimal = Integer.parseInt(binary, 2);
        System.out.println("Decimal: " + decimal);
    }
}
```

Output:

Decimal: 10

63. CONVERT DECIMAL TO BINARY

```java
public class DecimalToBinary {
    public static void main(String[] args) {
        int decimal = 10;
        String binary = Integer.toBinaryString(decimal);
        System.out.println("Binary: " + binary);
    }
}
```

Output:

Binary: 1010

64. CONVERT DECIMAL TO HEXADECIMAL

```java
public class DecimalToHexadecimal {
    public static void main(String[] args) {
        int decimal = 255;
        String hex = Integer.toHexString(decimal);
        System.out.println("Hexadecimal: " + hex);
    }
}
```

Output:

Hexadecimal: ff

65. CONVERT HEXADECIMAL TO DECIMAL

```java
public class HexadecimalToDecimal {
    public static void main(String[] args) {
        String hex = "ff";
        int decimal = Integer.parseInt(hex, 16);
        System.out.println("Decimal: " + decimal);
    }
}
```

Output:

Decimal: 255

66. SWAP TWO NUMBERS USING A TEMPORARY VARIABLE

```java
public class SwapNumbers {
    public static void main(String[] args) {
        int a = 5, b = 10;
        int temp = a;
        a = b;
        b = temp;
        System.out.println("After swapping: a = " + a + ", b = " + b);
    }
}
```

Output:

After swapping: a = 10, b = 5

67. SWAP TWO NUMBERS WITHOUT USING A TEMPORARY VARIABLE

```java
public class SwapNumbersWithoutTemp {
    public static void main(String[] args) {
        int a = 5, b = 10;
        a = a + b;
        b = a - b;
        a = a - b;
        System.out.println("After swapping: a = " + a + ", b = " + b);
    }
}
```

Output:

After swapping: a = 10, b = 5

68. REVERSE A NUMBER

```java
public class ReverseNumber {
    public static void main(String[] args) {
        int num = 1234, reversed = 0;
        while (num != 0) {
            int digit = num % 10;
            reversed = reversed * 10 + digit;
            num /= 10;
        }
        System.out.println("Reversed number: " + reversed);
    }
}
```

Output:

Reversed number: 4321

69. CHECK IF A NUMBER IS AN ARMSTRONG NUMBER

```java
public class ArmstrongNumber {
    public static void main(String[] args) {
        int num = 153, originalNum, remainder, result = 0;
        originalNum = num;
        while (originalNum != 0) {
            remainder = originalNum % 10;
            result += Math.pow(remainder, 3);
            originalNum /= 10;
        }
        if (result == num) {
            System.out.println(num + " is an Armstrong number.");
        } else {
            System.out.println(num + " is not an Armstrong number.");
        }
```

    }
}

Output:

153 is an Armstrong number.

70. CHECK IF A NUMBER IS A PRIME NUMBER

```java
public class PrimeNumber {
    public static void main(String[] args) {
        int num = 29;
        boolean isPrime = true;
        for (int i = 2; i <= num / 2; i++) {
            if (num % i == 0) {
                isPrime = false;
                break;
            }
        }
        if (isPrime) {
            System.out.println(num + " is a prime number.");
        } else {
            System.out.println(num + " is not a prime number.");
        }
```

}
}

Output:

29 is a prime number.

71. FIND THE LCM OF TWO NUMBERS

```java
public class LCM {
    public static void main(String[] args) {
        int num1 = 72, num2 = 120, lcm;
        lcm = (num1 > num2) ? num1 : num2;
        while (true) {
            if (lcm % num1 == 0 && lcm % num2 == 0) {
                System.out.println("LCM of " + num1 + " and " + num2 + " is: " + lcm);
                break;
            }
            lcm++;
        }
    }
}
```

Output:

LCM of 72 and 120 is: 360

72. FIND THE HCF OF TWO NUMBERS

```java
public class HCF {
    public static void main(String[] args) {
        int num1 = 72, num2 = 120, hcf = 1;
        for (int i = 1; i <= num1 && i <= num2; i++) {
            if (num1 % i == 0 && num2 % i == 0) {
                hcf = i;
            }
        }
        System.out.println("HCF of " + num1 + " and " + num2 + " is: " + hcf);
    }
}
```

Output:

HCF of 72 and 120 is: 24

73. CHECK IF A NUMBER IS EVEN OR ODD

```java
public class EvenOrOdd {
    public static void main(String[] args) {
        int num = 29;
        if (num % 2 == 0) {
            System.out.println(num + " is even.");
        } else {
            System.out.println(num + " is odd.");
        }
    }
}
```

Output:

29 is odd.

74. GENERATE A RANDOM NUMBER

```java
import java.util.Random;

public class RandomNumber {
    public static void main(String[] args) {
        Random rand = new Random();
        int randomNum = rand.nextInt(100);
        System.out.println("Random number: " + randomNum);
    }
}
```

Output:

Random number: [some random number between 0 and 99]

75. FIND THE GCD OF TWO NUMBERS USING THE EUCLIDEAN ALGORITHM

```java
public class EuclideanGCD {
    public static void main(String[] args) {
        int num1 = 56, num2 = 98;
        while (num1 != num2) {
            if (num1 > num2) {
                num1 -= num2;
            } else {
                num2 -= num1;
            }
        }
        System.out.println("GCD: " + num1);
    }
}
```

Output:

GCD: 14

76. FIND THE SQUARE ROOT OF A NUMBER

```java
public class SquareRoot {
    public static void main(String[] args) {
        double num = 25;
        double sqrt = Math.sqrt(num);
        System.out.println("Square root of " + num + " is: " + sqrt);
    }
}
```

Output:

Square root of 25 is: 5.0

77. CHECK IF A NUMBER IS A PERFECT SQUARE

```java
public class PerfectSquare {
    public static void main(String[] args) {
        int num = 16;
        double sqrt = Math.sqrt(num);
        if (sqrt == Math.floor(sqrt)) {
            System.out.println(num + " is a perfect square.");
        } else {
            System.out.println(num + " is not a perfect square.");
        }
    }
}
```

Output:

16 is a perfect square.

78. CHECK IF A NUMBER IS A PALINDROME

```java
public class PalindromeNumber {
    public static void main(String[] args) {
        int num = 121, reversed = 0, originalNum = num;
        while (num != 0) {
            int digit = num % 10;
            reversed = reversed * 10 + digit;
            num /= 10;
        }
        if (originalNum == reversed) {
            System.out.println(originalNum + " is a palindrome.");
        } else {
            System.out.println(originalNum + " is not a palindrome.");
        }
    }
}
```

}

Output:

121 is a palindrome.

79. FIND THE SUM OF PRIME NUMBERS UP TO N

```java
public class SumOfPrimes {
    public static void main(String[] args) {
        int n = 10;
        int sum = 0;
        for (int i = 2; i <= n; i++) {
            if (isPrime(i)) {
                sum += i;
            }
        }
        System.out.println("Sum of prime numbers up to " + n + " is: " + sum);
    }

    public static boolean isPrime(int num) {
        for (int i = 2; i <= num / 2; i++) {
            if (num % i == 0) {
```

```
                return false;
            }
        }
        return true;
    }
}
```

Output:

Sum of prime numbers up to 10 is: 17

80. FIND THE SUM OF NATURAL NUMBERS UP TO N

```java
public class SumOfNaturalNumbers {
    public static void main(String[] args) {
        int n = 10;
        int sum = n * (n + 1) / 2;
        System.out.println("Sum of first " + n + " natural numbers is: " + sum);
    }
}
```

Output:

Sum of first 10 natural numbers is: 55

81. CONVERT A CHARACTER TO ITS ASCII VALUE

```java
public class CharToASCII {
    public static void main(String[] args) {
        char ch = 'A';
        int ascii = (int) ch;
        System.out.println("ASCII value of " + ch + " is: " + ascii);
    }
}
```

Output:

ASCII value of A is: 65

82. FIND THE SUM OF EVEN AND ODD NUMBERS IN AN ARRAY

```java
public class SumEvenOddArray {
    public static void main(String[] args) {
        int[] array = {1, 2, 3, 4, 5};
        int sumEven = 0, sumOdd = 0;
        for (int num : array) {
            if (num % 2 == 0) {
                sumEven += num;
            } else {
                sumOdd += num;
            }
        }
        System.out.println("Sum of even numbers: " + sumEven);
        System.out.println("Sum of odd numbers: " + sumOdd);
    }
}
```

Output:

Sum of even numbers: 6

Sum of odd numbers: 9

83. FIND THE PRODUCT OF ARRAY ELEMENTS

```java
public class ProductOfArray {
    public static void main(String[] args) {
        int[] array = {1, 2, 3, 4, 5};
        int product = 1;
        for (int num : array) {
            product *= num;
        }
        System.out.println("Product of array elements: " + product);
    }
}
```

Output:

Product of array elements: 120

84. FIND THE LARGEST AND SMALLEST ELEMENTS IN AN ARRAY

```java
public class LargestSmallestArray {
    public static void main(String[] args) {
        int[] array = {1, 2, 3, 4, 5};
        int largest = array[0], smallest = array[0];
        for (int num : array) {
            if (num > largest) {
                largest = num;
            }
            if (num < smallest) {
                smallest = num;
            }
        }
        System.out.println("Largest element: " + largest);
        System.out.println("Smallest element: " + smallest);
    }
```

}

Output:

Largest element: 5

Smallest element: 1

85. COUNT THE NUMBER OF DIGITS IN A NUMBER

```java
public class CountDigits {
    public static void main(String[] args) {
        int num = 12345;
        int count = 0;
        while (num != 0) {
            num /= 10;
            count++;
        }
        System.out.println("Number of digits: " + count);
    }
}
```

Output:

Number of digits: 5

86. PRINT THE MULTIPLICATION TABLE FOR A NUMBER

```
public class MultiplicationTable {
    public static void main(String[] args) {
        int num = 5;
        for (int i = 1; i <= 10; i++) {
            System.out.println(num + " x " + i + " = " + (num * i));
        }
    }
}
```

Output:

5 x 1 = 5

5 x 2 = 10

5 x 3 = 15

5 x 4 = 20

5 x 5 = 25

5 x 6 = 30

5 x 7 = 35

5 x 8 = 40

5 x 9 = 45

5 x 10 = 50

87. FIND THE SUM OF THE DIAGONALS IN A MATRIX

```java
public class SumOfDiagonals {
    public static void main(String[] args) {
        int[][] matrix = {
            {1, 2, 3},
            {4, 5, 6},
            {7, 8, 9}
        };
        int primaryDiagonal = 0, secondaryDiagonal = 0;
        for (int i = 0; i < matrix.length; i++) {
            primaryDiagonal += matrix[i][i];
            secondaryDiagonal += matrix[i][matrix.length - i - 1];
        }
        System.out.println("Sum of primary diagonal: " + primaryDiagonal);
```

```
    System.out.println("Sum of secondary diagonal: " + secondaryDiagonal);
  }
}
```

Output:

Sum of primary diagonal: 15

Sum of secondary diagonal: 15

88. FIND THE TRANSPOSE OF A MATRIX

```java
public class TransposeMatrix {
    public static void main(String[] args) {
        int[][] matrix = {
            {1, 2, 3},
            {4, 5, 6},
            {7, 8, 9}
        };
        int[][] transpose = new int[matrix[0].length][matrix.length];
        for (int i = 0; i < matrix.length; i++) {
            for (int j = 0; j < matrix[0].length; j++) {
                transpose[j][i] = matrix[i][j];
            }
        }
        System.out.println("Transpose of the matrix:");
```

```
            for (int[] row : transpose) {
                for (int val : row) {
                    System.out.print(val + " ");
                }
                System.out.println();
            }
        }
    }
```

Output:

Transpose of the matrix:

1 4 7

2 5 8

3 6 9

89. PRINT THE FIBONACCI SERIES WITHOUT RECURSION

```java
public class FibonacciWithoutRecursion {
    public static void main(String[] args) {
        int count = 10, num1 = 0, num2 = 1;
        System.out.print("Fibonacci Series: " + num1 + " " + num2);
        for (int i = 2; i < count; ++i) {
            int num3 = num1 + num2;
            System.out.print(" " + num3);
            num1 = num2;
            num2 = num3;
        }
    }
}
```

Output:

Fibonacci Series: 0 1 1 2 3 5 8 13 21 34

90. IMPLEMENT A BASIC CALCULATOR

```java
import java.util.Scanner;
public class BasicCalculator {
    public static void main(String[] args) {
        Scanner scanner = new Scanner(System.in);
        System.out.print("Enter first number: ");
        double num1 = scanner.nextDouble();
        System.out.print("Enter second number: ");
        double num2 = scanner.nextDouble();
        System.out.print("Enter operator (+, -, *, /): ");
        char operator = scanner.next().charAt(0);

        double result = 0;
```

```java
switch (operator) {
    case '+':
        result = num1 + num2;
        break;
    case '-':
        result = num1 - num2;
        break;
    case '*':
        result = num1 * num2;
        break;
    case '/':
        if (num2 != 0) {
            result = num1 / num2;
        } else {
            System.out.println("Cannot divide by zero");
            return;
        }
        break;
```

```java
            default:
                System.out.println("Invalid operator");
                return;
        }
        System.out.println("Result: " + result);
    }
}
```

Output:

Enter first number: 10

Enter second number: 5

Enter operator (+, -, *, /): /

Result: 2.0

91. CHECK IF TWO STRINGS ARE ANAGRAMS

```java
import java.util.Arrays;

public class AnagramCheck {

    public static void main(String[] args) {

        String str1 = "listen";

        String str2 = "silent";


        if (isAnagram(str1, str2)) {

            System.out.println(str1 + " and " + str2 + " are anagrams.");

        } else {

            System.out.println(str1 + " and " + str2 + " are not anagrams.");

        }

    }


    public static boolean isAnagram(String str1, String str2) {
```

```java
        if (str1.length() != str2.length()) {
            return false;
        }
        char[] arr1 = str1.toCharArray();
        char[] arr2 = str2.toCharArray();
        Arrays.sort(arr1);
        Arrays.sort(arr2);
        return Arrays.equals(arr1, arr2);
    }
}
```

Output:

listen and silent are anagrams.

92. FIND THE FACTORIAL OF A NUMBER USING RECURSION

```java
public class FactorialRecursion {
    public static void main(String[] args) {
        int num = 5;
        int result = factorial(num);
        System.out.println("Factorial of " + num + " is: " + result);
    }

    public static int factorial(int n) {
        if (n == 0) {
            return 1;
        }
        return n * factorial(n - 1);
    }
}
```

Output:

Factorial of 5 is: 120

93. CALCULATE THE POWER OF A NUMBER USING A LOOP

```java
public class PowerLoop {
    public static void main(String[] args) {
        int base = 2, exponent = 4;
        int result = 1;
        for (int i = 0; i < exponent; i++) {
            result *= base;
        }
        System.out.println(base + "^" + exponent + " = " + result);
    }
}
```

Output:

2^4 = 16

94. FIND THE SUM OF NATURAL NUMBERS USING RECURSION

```java
public class SumNaturalRecursion {
    public static void main(String[] args) {
        int n = 10;
        int sum = sum(n);
        System.out.println("Sum of first " + n + " natural numbers is: " + sum);
    }

    public static int sum(int n) {
        if (n == 1) {
            return n;
        }
        return n + sum(n - 1);
    }
}
```

Output:

Sum of first 10 natural numbers is: 55

95. FIND THE FIBONACCI SERIES USING RECURSION

```java
public class FibonacciRecursion {
    public static void main(String[] args) {
        int n = 10;
        System.out.print("Fibonacci Series: ");
        for (int i = 0; i < n; i++) {
            System.out.print(fibonacci(i) + " ");
        }
    }
    public static int fibonacci(int n) {
        if (n <= 1) {
            return n;
        }
        return fibonacci(n - 1) + fibonacci(n - 2);
    }
}
```

Output:

Fibonacci Series: 0 1 1 2 3 5 8 13 21 34

96. CALCULATE THE SUM OF DIGITS OF A NUMBER USING RECURSION

```java
public class SumOfDigitsRecursion {
    public static void main(String[] args) {
        int num = 1234;
        int sum = sumOfDigits(num);
        System.out.println("Sum of digits: " + sum);
    }
    public static int sumOfDigits(int num) {
        if (num == 0) {
            return 0;
        }
        return num % 10 + sumOfDigits(num / 10);
    }
}
```

Output:

Sum of digits: 10

97. REVERSE A STRING USING RECURSION

```java
public class ReverseStringRecursion {
    public static void main(String[] args) {
        String str = "Hello";
        String reversed = reverseString(str);
        System.out.println("Reversed string: " + reversed);
    }
    public static String reverseString(String str) {
        if (str.isEmpty()) {
            return str;
        }
        return reverseString(str.substring(1)) + str.charAt(0);
    }
}
```

Output:

Reversed string: olleH

98. CALCULATE THE GREATEST COMMON DIVISOR (GCD) USING RECURSION

```java
public class GCDRecursion {
    public static void main(String[] args) {
        int num1 = 56, num2 = 98;
        int gcd = gcd(num1, num2);
        System.out.println("GCD: " + gcd);
    }
    public static int gcd(int a, int b) {
        if (b == 0) {
            return a;
        }
        return gcd(b, a % b);
    }
}
```

Output:

GCD: 14

99. PRINT ALL PRIME NUMBERS UP TO N USING A METHOD

```java
public class PrimeNumbers {

    public static void main(String[] args) {

        int n = 50;

        System.out.print("Prime numbers up to " + n + ": ");

        for (int i = 2; i <= n; i++) {

            if (isPrime(i)) {

                System.out.print(i + " ");

            }

        }

    }


    public static boolean isPrime(int num) {

        for (int i = 2; i <= Math.sqrt(num); i++) {

            if (num % i == 0) {

                return false;
```

            }
        }
        return true;
    }
}

Output:

Prime numbers up to 50: 2 3 5 7 11 13 17 19 23 29 31 37 41 43 47

100. FIND THE LENGTH OF A STRING WITHOUT USING LENGTH() METHOD

```java
public class StringLength {
    public static void main(String[] args) {
        String str = "Hello, World!";
        int length = 0;
        for (char c : str.toCharArray()) {
            length++;
        }
        System.out.println("Length of the string: " + length);
    }
}
```

Output:

Length of the string: 13

101. FIND THE FIRST NON-REPEATED CHARACTER IN A STRING

```java
import java.util.LinkedHashMap;
import java.util.Map;

public class FirstNonRepeatedCharacter {
    public static void main(String[] args) {
        String str = "swiss";
        char result = firstNonRepeatedChar(str);
        if (result != 0) {
            System.out.println("First non-repeated character: " + result);
        } else {
            System.out.println("All characters are repeated.");
        }
    }
```

```java
public static char firstNonRepeatedChar(String str) {

    Map<Character, Integer> charCount = new LinkedHashMap<>();

    for (char c : str.toCharArray()) {

        charCount.put(c, charCount.getOrDefault(c, 0) + 1);

    }

    for (Map.Entry<Character, Integer> entry : charCount.entrySet()) {

        if (entry.getValue() == 1) {

            return entry.getKey();

        }

    }

    return 0;

  }

}
```

Output:

First non-repeated character: w

102. CHECK IF A NUMBER IS A PALINDROME USING RECURSION

```java
public class PalindromeCheckRecursion {
    public static void main(String[] args) {
        int num = 121;
        boolean isPalindrome = isPalindrome(num, 0, String.valueOf(num).length() - 1);
        System.out.println(num + " is palindrome: " + isPalindrome);
    }

    public static boolean isPalindrome(int num, int start, int end) {
        String str = String.valueOf(num);
        if (start >= end) {
            return true;
        }
        if (str.charAt(start) != str.charAt(end)) {
```

```
            return false;
        }
        return isPalindrome(num, start + 1, end - 1);
    }
}
```

Output:

121 is palindrome: true

103. COUNT THE NUMBER OF WORDS IN A STRING

```java
public class WordCount {
    public static void main(String[] args) {
        String str = "Hello, how are you?";
        String[] words = str.split("\\s+");
        System.out.println("Number of words: " + words.length);
    }
}
```

Output:

Number of words: 4

104. FIND THE SECOND LARGEST NUMBER IN AN ARRAY

```java
public class SecondLargest {
    public static void main(String[] args) {
        int[] array = {1, 2, 3, 4, 5};
        int largest = Integer.MIN_VALUE, secondLargest = Integer.MIN_VALUE;
        for (int num : array) {
            if (num > largest) {
                secondLargest = largest;
                largest = num;
            } else if (num > secondLargest && num != largest) {
                secondLargest = num;
            }
        }
        System.out.println("Second largest number: " + secondLargest);
    }
}
```

}

Output:

Second largest number: 4

105. CALCULATE THE SUM OF ALL PRIME NUMBERS IN AN ARRAY

```java
public class SumOfPrimesInArray {
    public static void main(String[] args) {
        int[] array = {1, 2, 3, 4, 5, 6, 7, 8, 9, 10};
        int sum = 0;
        for (int num : array) {
            if (isPrime(num)) {
                sum += num;
            }
        }
        System.out.println("Sum of prime numbers: " + sum);
    }

    public static boolean isPrime(int num) {
        if (num <= 1) {
            return false;
```

```
    }
    for (int i = 2; i <= Math.sqrt(num); i++)
{
        if (num % i == 0) {
            return false;
        }
    }
    return true;
  }
}
```

Output:

Sum of prime numbers: 17

106. REPLACE ALL VOWELS IN A STRING WITH A SPECIFIC CHARACTER

```java
public class ReplaceVowels {
    public static void main(String[] args) {
        String str = "Hello World";
        char replaceChar = '*';
        String result = str.replaceAll("[AEIOUaeiou]", String.valueOf(replaceChar));
        System.out.println("Modified string: " + result);
    }
}
```

Output:

Modified string: H*ll* W*rld

107. FIND THE LARGEST PALINDROME IN AN ARRAY

```java
public class LargestPalindromeInArray {
    public static void main(String[] args) {
        int[] array = {123, 121, 545, 999, 1001, 12321};
        int largestPalindrome = 0;
        for (int num : array) {
            if (isPalindrome(num) && num > largestPalindrome) {
                largestPalindrome = num;
            }
        }
        System.out.println("Largest palindrome: " + largestPalindrome);
    }

    public static boolean isPalindrome(int num) {
```

```
        int original = num, reverse = 0;
        while (num != 0) {
            int digit = num % 10;
            reverse = reverse * 10 + digit;
            num /= 10;
        }
        return original == reverse;
    }
}
```

Output:

Largest palindrome: 12321

108. COUNT THE NUMBER OF VOWELS AND CONSONANTS IN A STRING

```java
public class CountVowelsConsonants {
    public static void main(String[] args) {
        String str = "Hello World";
        int vowels = 0, consonants = 0;
        str = str.toLowerCase();
        for (char c : str.toCharArray()) {
            if (c >= 'a' && c <= 'z') {
                if (c == 'a' || c == 'e' || c == 'i' || c == 'o' || c == 'u') {
                    vowels++;
                } else {
                    consonants++;
                }
            }
        }
```

```java
        System.out.println("Number of vowels: " + vowels);
        System.out.println("Number of consonants: " + consonants);
    }
}
```

Output:

Number of vowels: 3

Number of consonants: 7

109. CHECK IF A NUMBER IS AN ARMSTRONG NUMBER

```java
public class ArmstrongNumber {
    public static void main(String[] args) {
        int num = 153;
        if (isArmstrong(num)) {
            System.out.println(num + " is an Armstrong number.");
        } else {
            System.out.println(num + " is not an Armstrong number.");
        }
    }


    public static boolean isArmstrong(int num) {
        int original = num, result = 0;
        int n = String.valueOf(num).length();
        while (num != 0) {
```

```
        int digit = num % 10;
        result += Math.pow(digit, n);
        num /= 10;
    }
    return original == result;
  }
}
```

Output:

153 is an Armstrong number.

110. CONVERT A DECIMAL NUMBER TO BINARY

```java
public class DecimalToBinary {
    public static void main(String[] args) {
        int num = 10;
        String binary = Integer.toBinaryString(num);
        System.out.println("Binary of " + num + " is: " + binary);
    }
}
```

Output:

Binary of 10 is: 1010

111. CONVERT A BINARY NUMBER TO DECIMAL

```java
public class BinaryToDecimal {
    public static void main(String[] args) {
        String binary = "1010";
        int decimal = Integer.parseInt(binary, 2);
        System.out.println("Decimal of " + binary + " is: " + decimal);
    }
}
```

Output:

Decimal of 1010 is: 10

112. CONVERT A DECIMAL NUMBER TO HEXADECIMAL

```java
public class DecimalToHexadecimal {
    public static void main(String[] args) {
        int num = 255;
        String hex = Integer.toHexString(num);
        System.out.println("Hexadecimal of " + num + " is: " + hex.toUpperCase());
    }
}
```

Output:

Hexadecimal of 255 is: FF

113. CONVERT A HEXADECIMAL NUMBER TO DECIMAL

```java
public class HexadecimalToDecimal {
    public static void main(String[] args) {
        String hex = "FF";
        int decimal = Integer.parseInt(hex, 16);
        System.out.println("Decimal of " + hex + " is: " + decimal);
    }
}
```

Output:

Decimal of FF is: 255

114. FIND THE HCF AND LCM OF TWO NUMBERS

```java
public class HCFAndLCM {
    public static void main(String[] args) {
        int num1 = 12, num2 = 18;
        int hcf = gcd(num1, num2);
        int lcm = (num1 * num2) / hcf;
        System.out.println("HCF: " + hcf);
        System.out.println("LCM: " + lcm);
    }
    public static int gcd(int a, int b) {
        if (b == 0) {
            return a; }
        return gcd(b, a % b); }
}
```

Output:

HCF: 6

LCM: 36

115. REVERSE A NUMBER USING RECURSION

```java
public class ReverseNumberRecursion {
    public static void main(String[] args) {
        int num = 1234;
        int reversed = reverse(num);
        System.out.println("Reversed number: " + reversed);
    }
    public static int reverse(int num) {
        String str = Integer.toString(num);
        if (str.length() == 1) {
            return num; }
        return Integer.parseInt(str.charAt(str.length() - 1) + "" + reverse(Integer.parseInt(str.substring(0, str.length() - 1)))); }
}
```

Output: Reversed number: 4321

116. FIND THE SUM OF EVEN NUMBERS IN AN ARRAY

```java
public class SumOfEvenNumbers {
    public static void main(String[] args) {
        int[] array = {1, 2, 3, 4, 5, 6};
        int sum = 0;
        for (int num : array) {
            if (num % 2 == 0) {
                sum += num;
            }
        }
        System.out.println("Sum of even numbers: " + sum);
    }
}
```

Output:

Sum of even numbers: 12

117. CHECK IF A STRING IS A PALINDROME USING A LOOP

```java
public class PalindromeCheckLoop {
    public static void main(String[] args) {
        String str = "madam";
        boolean isPalindrome = true;
        int n = str.length();

        for (int i = 0; i < n / 2; i++) {
            if (str.charAt(i) != str.charAt(n - i - 1)) {
                isPalindrome = false;
                break;
            }
        }

        System.out.println(str + " is palindrome: " + isPalindrome);
    }
```

}

Output:

madam is palindrome: true

118. FIND THE NUMBER OF DIGITS IN AN INTEGER

```java
public class NumberOfDigits {
    public static void main(String[] args) {
        int num = 123456;
        int count = 0;

        while (num != 0) {
            num /= 10;
            count++;
        }

        System.out.println("Number of digits: " + count);
    }
}
```

Output:

Number of digits: 6

119. GENERATE A MULTIPLICATION TABLE FOR A GIVEN NUMBER

```java
public class MultiplicationTable {
    public static void main(String[] args) {
        int num = 5;

        for (int i = 1; i <= 10; i++) {
            System.out.println(num + " * " + i + " = " + num * i);
        }
    }
}
```

Output:

5 * 1 = 5

5 * 2 = 10

5 * 3 = 15

5 * 4 = 20

5 * 5 = 25

5 * 6 = 30

5 * 7 = 35

5 * 8 = 40

5 * 9 = 45

5 * 10 = 50

120. CALCULATE THE AREA OF A RECTANGLE

```java
public class AreaOfRectangle {
    public static void main(String[] args) {
        int length = 10;
        int breadth = 5;
        int area = length * breadth;
        System.out.println("Area of rectangle: " + area);
    }
}
```

Output:

Area of rectangle: 50

121. CHECK IF A NUMBER IS EVEN OR ODD

```java
public class EvenOddCheck {
    public static void main(String[] args) {
        int num = 7;

        if (num % 2 == 0) {
            System.out.println(num + " is even.");
        } else {
            System.out.println(num + " is odd.");
        }
    }
}
```

Output:

7 is odd.

122. FIND THE SMALLEST NUMBER IN AN ARRAY

```java
public class SmallestNumber {
    public static void main(String[] args) {
        int[] array = {3, 1, 4, 1, 5, 9};
        int smallest = array[0];

        for (int num : array) {
            if (num < smallest) {
                smallest = num;
            }
        }

        System.out.println("Smallest number: " + smallest);
    }
}
```

Output:

Smallest number: 1

123. CONVERT CELSIUS TO FAHRENHEIT

```java
public class CelsiusToFahrenheit {
    public static void main(String[] args) {
        double celsius = 25;
        double fahrenheit = (celsius * 9/5) + 32;
        System.out.println(celsius + "°C = " + fahrenheit + "°F");
    }
}
```

Output:

25.0°C = 77.0°F

124. FIND THE SUM OF ODD NUMBERS IN AN ARRAY

```java
public class SumOfOddNumbers {
    public static void main(String[] args) {
        int[] array = {1, 2, 3, 4, 5, 6};
        int sum = 0;
        for (int num : array) {
            if (num % 2 != 0) {
                sum += num;
            }
        }
        System.out.println("Sum of odd numbers: " + sum);
    }
}
```

Output:

Sum of odd numbers: 9

125. CHECK IF A YEAR IS A LEAP YEAR

```java
public class LeapYearCheck {
    public static void main(String[] args) {
        int year = 2020;

        if ((year % 4 == 0 && year % 100 != 0) || (year % 400 == 0)) {
            System.out.println(year + " is a leap year.");
        } else {
            System.out.println(year + " is not a leap year.");
        }
    }
}
```

Output:

2020 is a leap year.

126. CALCULATE THE AREA OF A CIRCLE

```java
public class AreaOfCircle {
    public static void main(String[] args) {
        double radius = 7;
        double area = Math.PI * radius * radius;
        System.out.println("Area of circle: " + area);
    }
}
```

Output:

Area of circle: 153.93804002589985

127. CALCULATE THE AREA OF A TRIANGLE

```java
public class AreaOfTriangle {
    public static void main(String[] args) {
        double base = 5;
        double height = 10;
        double area = 0.5 * base * height;
        System.out.println("Area of triangle: " + area);
    }
}
```

Output:

Area of triangle: 25.0

128. FIND THE GCD OF TWO NUMBERS USING A LOOP

```java
public class GCDLoop {
    public static void main(String[] args) {
        int num1 = 56;
        int num2 = 98;
        int gcd = 1;
        for (int i = 1; i <= num1 && i <= num2; i++) {
            if (num1 % i == 0 && num2 % i == 0) {
                gcd = i;
            }
        }
        System.out.println("GCD: " + gcd);
    }
}
```

Output:

GCD: 14

129. CALCULATE THE LCM OF TWO NUMBERS USING A LOOP

```java
public class LCMLoop {
    public static void main(String[] args) {
        int num1 = 12;
        int num2 = 15;
        int lcm = (num1 > num2) ? num1 : num2;
        while (true) {
            if (lcm % num1 == 0 && lcm % num2 == 0) {
                System.out.println("LCM: " + lcm);
                break; }
            lcm++;
        }
    }
}
```

Output:

LCM: 60

130. FIND THE MAXIMUM AND MINIMUM VALUES IN AN ARRAY

```java
public class MaxMinInArray {
    public static void main(String[] args) {
        int[] array = {5, 3, 9, 1, 6};
        int max = array[0];
        int min = array[0];

        for (int num : array) {
            if (num > max) {
                max = num;
            }
            if (num < min) {
                min = num;
            }
        }
```

```java
        System.out.println("Maximum value: " + max);
        System.out.println("Minimum value: " + min);
    }
}
```

Output:

Maximum value: 9

Minimum value: 1

131. CALCULATE THE PERIMETER OF A RECTANGLE

```java
public class PerimeterOfRectangle {
    public static void main(String[] args) {
        int length = 10;
        int breadth = 5;
        int perimeter = 2 * (length + breadth);
        System.out.println("Perimeter of rectangle: " + perimeter);
    }
}
```

Output:

Perimeter of rectangle: 30

132. SWAP TWO NUMBERS WITHOUT USING A TEMPORARY VARIABLE

```java
public class SwapNumbers {
    public static void main(String[] args) {
        int a = 5, b = 3;
        System.out.println("Before swap: a = " + a + ", b = " + b);

        a = a + b;
        b = a - b;
        a = a - b;

        System.out.println("After swap: a = " + a + ", b = " + b);
    }
}
```

Output:

Before swap: a = 5, b = 3

After swap: a = 3, b = 5

133. FIND THE SECOND SMALLEST NUMBER IN AN ARRAY

```java
import java.util.Arrays;

public class SecondSmallestNumber {
    public static void main(String[] args) {
        int[] array = {5, 2, 9, 1, 5, 6};
        Arrays.sort(array);
        System.out.println("Second smallest number: " + array[1]);
    }
}
```

Output:

Second smallest number: 2

134. FIND THE LENGTH OF A STRING

```java
public class LengthOfString {
    public static void main(String[] args) {
        String str = "Hello, world!";
        System.out.println("Length of string: " + str.length());
    }
}
```

Output:

Length of string: 13

135. COUNT THE NUMBER OF WORDS IN A STRING

```java
public class WordCount {
    public static void main(String[] args) {
        String str = "Java is fun to learn";
        String[] words = str.split(" ");
        System.out.println("Number of words: " + words.length);
    }
}
```

Output:

Number of words: 5

136. CALCULATE THE SQUARE ROOT OF A NUMBER

```java
public class SquareRoot {
    public static void main(String[] args) {
        int num = 16;
        double sqrt = Math.sqrt(num);
        System.out.println("Square root of " + num + " is: " + sqrt);
    }
}
```

Output:

Square root of 16 is: 4.0

137. CONVERT A STRING TO UPPERCASE

```java
public class StringToUppercase {
    public static void main(String[] args) {
        String str = "hello world";
        String upperStr = str.toUpperCase();
        System.out.println("Uppercase string: " + upperStr);
    }
}
```

Output:

Uppercase string: HELLO WORLD

138. CONVERT A STRING TO LOWERCASE

```java
public class StringToLowercase {
    public static void main(String[] args) {
        String str = "HELLO WORLD";
        String lowerStr = str.toLowerCase();
        System.out.println("Lowercase string: " + lowerStr);
    }
}
```

Output:

Lowercase string: hello world

139. REVERSE A STRING USING A LOOP

```java
public class ReverseStringLoop {
    public static void main(String[] args) {
        String str = "Java";
        String reversed = "";

        for (int i = str.length() - 1; i >= 0; i--) {
            reversed += str.charAt(i);
        }

        System.out.println("Reversed string: " + reversed);
    }
}
```

Output:

Reversed string: avaJ

140. CALCULATE THE FACTORIAL OF A NUMBER USING RECURSION

```java
public class FactorialRecursion {

    public static void main(String[] args) {

        int num = 5;

        int result = factorial(num);

        System.out.println("Factorial of " + num + " is: " + result);

    }


    public static int factorial(int num) {

        if (num == 0) {

            return 1;

        }

        return num * factorial(num - 1);

    }
}
```

Output:

Factorial of 5 is: 120

141. COUNT THE FREQUENCY OF EACH CHARACTER IN A STRING

```java
import java.util.HashMap;

public class CharacterFrequency {
    public static void main(String[] args) {
        String str = "hello world";
        HashMap<Character, Integer> freqMap = new HashMap<>();

        for (char c : str.toCharArray()) {
            freqMap.put(c, freqMap.getOrDefault(c, 0) + 1);
        }

        for (char c : freqMap.keySet()) {
            System.out.println(c + ": " + freqMap.get(c));
        }
```

        }
}

Output:

h: 1

e: 1

l: 3

o: 2

 : 1

w: 1

r: 1

d: 1

142. FIND THE FIRST NON-REPEATED CHARACTER IN A STRING

```java
import java.util.LinkedHashMap;
import java.util.Map;

public class FirstNonRepeatedCharacter {
    public static void main(String[] args) {
        String str = "swiss";
        LinkedHashMap<Character, Integer> charCount = new LinkedHashMap<>();

        for (char c : str.toCharArray()) {
            charCount.put(c, charCount.getOrDefault(c, 0) + 1);
        }

        for (Map.Entry<Character, Integer> entry : charCount.entrySet()) {
            if (entry.getValue() == 1) {
```

```java
            System.out.println("First non-repeated character: " + entry.getKey());
            break;
        }
    }
  }
}
```

Output:

First non-repeated character: w

143. GENERATE FIBONACCI SERIES UP TO N TERMS

```java
public class FibonacciSeries {
    public static void main(String[] args) {
        int n = 10;
        int a = 0, b = 1;
        System.out.print("Fibonacci series: " + a + ", " + b);
        for (int i = 2; i < n; i++) {
            int next = a + b;
            System.out.print(", " + next);
            a = b;
            b = next;
        }
    }
}
```

Output:

Fibonacci series: 0, 1, 1, 2, 3, 5, 8, 13, 21, 34

144. FIND THE NTH FIBONACCI NUMBER USING RECURSION

```java
public class NthFibonacci {
    public static void main(String[] args) {
        int n = 7;
        System.out.println("Nth Fibonacci number: " + fibonacci(n));
    }
    public static int fibonacci(int n) {
        if (n <= 1) {
            return n;
        }
        return fibonacci(n - 1) + fibonacci(n - 2);
    }
}
```

Output:

Nth Fibonacci number: 13

145. REMOVE DUPLICATES FROM AN ARRAY

```java
import java.util.HashSet;
public class RemoveDuplicates {
    public static void main(String[] args) {
        int[] array = {1, 2, 3, 1, 2, 4, 5};
        HashSet<Integer> set = new HashSet<>();

        for (int num : array) {
            set.add(num);
        }
        System.out.println("Array after removing duplicates: " + set);
    }
}
```

Output:

Array after removing duplicates: [1, 2, 3, 4, 5]

146. CHECK IF TWO STRINGS ARE ANAGRAMS

```java
import java.util.Arrays;

public class AnagramCheck {
    public static void main(String[] args) {
        String str1 = "listen";
        String str2 = "silent";

        if (isAnagram(str1, str2)) {
            System.out.println(str1 + " and " + str2 + " are anagrams.");
        } else {
            System.out.println(str1 + " and " + str2 + " are not anagrams.");
        }
    }
```

```java
    public static boolean isAnagram(String str1, String str2) {
        char[] arr1 = str1.toCharArray();
        char[] arr2 = str2.toCharArray();
        Arrays.sort(arr1);
        Arrays.sort(arr2);
        return Arrays.equals(arr1, arr2);
    }
}
```

Output:

listen and silent are anagrams.

147. REVERSE THE WORDS IN A SENTENCE

```java
public class ReverseWords {
    public static void main(String[] args) {
        String sentence = "Java is fun";
        String[] words = sentence.split(" ");
        StringBuilder reversedSentence = new StringBuilder();
        for (int i = words.length - 1; i >= 0; i--) {
            reversedSentence.append(words[i]).append(" ");
        }
        System.out.println("Reversed sentence: " + reversedSentence.toString().trim());
    }
}
```

Output:

Reversed sentence: fun is Java

148. CHECK IF A STRING IS A SUBSTRING OF ANOTHER STRING

```java
public class SubstringCheck {
    public static void main(String[] args) {
        String str1 = "hello";
        String str2 = "ell";

        if (str1.contains(str2)) {
            System.out.println(str2 + " is a substring of " + str1);
        } else {
            System.out.println(str2 + " is not a substring of " + str1);
        }
    }
}
```

Output:

ell is a substring of hello

149. FIND THE SUM OF THE DIAGONAL ELEMENTS IN A MATRIX

```java
public class DiagonalSum {
    public static void main(String[] args) {
        int[][] matrix = {
            {1, 2, 3},
            {4, 5, 6},
            {7, 8, 9}
        };
        int sum = 0;
        for (int i = 0; i < matrix.length; i++) {
            sum += matrix[i][i];
        }
        System.out.println("Sum of diagonal elements: " + sum);
    }
}
```

Output:

Sum of diagonal elements: 15

150. FIND THE SUM OF EACH ROW IN A MATRIX

```java
public class RowSum {
    public static void main(String[] args) {
        int[][] matrix = {
            {1, 2, 3},
            {4, 5, 6},
            {7, 8, 9}
        };

        for (int i = 0; i < matrix.length; i++) {
            int sum = 0;
            for (int j = 0; j < matrix[i].length; j++) {
                sum += matrix[i][j];
            }
            System.out.println("Sum of row " + (i + 1) + ": " + sum);
        }
```

    }
}

Output:

Sum of row 1: 6

Sum of row 2: 15

Sum of row 3: 24

151. FIND THE SUM OF EACH COLUMN IN A MATRIX

```java
public class ColumnSum {
    public static void main(String[] args) {
        int[][] matrix = {
            {1, 2, 3},
            {4, 5, 6},
            {7, 8, 9}
        };

        for (int i = 0; i < matrix[0].length; i++) {
            int sum = 0;
            for (int j = 0; j < matrix.length; j++) {
                sum += matrix[j][i];
            }
            System.out.println("Sum of column " + (i + 1) + ": " + sum);
```

            }
        }
}

Output:

Sum of column 1: 12

Sum of column 2: 15

Sum of column 3: 18

152. CHECK IF A MATRIX IS SYMMETRIC

```java
public class SymmetricMatrix {
    public static void main(String[] args) {
        int[][] matrix = {
            {1, 2, 3},
            {2, 5, 6},
            {3, 6, 9}
        };

        boolean isSymmetric = true;
        for (int i = 0; i < matrix.length; i++) {
            for (int j = 0; j < matrix[0].length; j++) {
                if (matrix[i][j] != matrix[j][i]) {
                    isSymmetric = false;
                    break;
                }
```

```
        }
    }


    if (isSymmetric) {
        System.out.println("The matrix is symmetric.");
    } else {
        System.out.println("The matrix is not symmetric.");
    }
  }
}
```

Output:

The matrix is symmetric.

153. FIND THE TRACE OF A MATRIX

```java
public class MatrixTrace {
    public static void main(String[] args) {
        int[][] matrix = {
            {1, 2, 3},
            {4, 5, 6},
            {7, 8, 9}
        };
        int trace = 0;
        for (int i = 0; i < matrix.length; i++) {
            trace += matrix[i][i];
        }
        System.out.println("Trace of the matrix: " + trace);
    }
}
```

Output:

Trace of the matrix: 15

154. ROTATE A MATRIX 90 DEGREES CLOCKWISE

```java
public class RotateMatrix {
    public static void main(String[] args) {
        int[][] matrix = {
            {1, 2, 3},
            {4, 5, 6},
            {7, 8, 9}
        };

        int n = matrix.length;
        int[][] rotatedMatrix = new int[n][n];

        for (int i = 0; i < n; i++) {
            for (int j = 0; j < n; j++) {
                rotatedMatrix[j][n - 1 - i] = matrix[i][j];
            }
```

```java
        }

        System.out.println("Rotated matrix:");
        for (int[] row : rotatedMatrix) {
            for (int val : row) {
                System.out.print(val + " ");
            }
            System.out.println();
        }
    }
}
```

Output:

Rotated matrix:

7 4 1

8 5 2

9 6 3

155. PRINT A PASCAL'S TRIANGLE

```java
public class PascalTriangle {
    public static void main(String[] args) {
        int n = 5;
        int[][] triangle = new int[n][n];

        for (int i = 0; i < n; i++) {
            for (int j = 0; j <= i; j++) {
                if (j == 0 || j == i) {
                    triangle[i][j] = 1;
                } else {
                    triangle[i][j] = triangle[i - 1][j - 1] + triangle[i - 1][j];
                }
                System.out.print(triangle[i][j] + " ");
            }
            System.out.println();
```

```
        }
    }
}
```

Output:

1
1 1
1 2 1
1 3 3 1
1 4 6 4 1

156. FIND THE GCD (GREATEST COMMON DIVISOR) OF TWO NUMBERS USING EUCLIDEAN ALGORITHM

```java
public class EuclideanGCD {
    public static void main(String[] args) {
        int num1 = 56;
        int num2 = 98;
        System.out.println("GCD of " + num1 + " and " + num2 + " is: " + gcd(num1, num2));
    }
    public static int gcd(int a, int b) {
        if (b == 0) {
            return a; }
        return gcd(b, a % b);
    }
}
```

Output:

GCD of 56 and 98 is: 14

157. IMPLEMENT BUBBLE SORT ALGORITHM

```java
import java.util.Arrays;

public class BubbleSort {
    public static void main(String[] args) {
        int[] array = {64, 34, 25, 12, 22, 11, 90};

        for (int i = 0; i < array.length - 1; i++) {
            for (int j = 0; j < array.length - i - 1; j++) {
                if (array[j] > array[j + 1]) {
                    int temp = array[j];
                    array[j] = array[j + 1];
                    array[j + 1] = temp;
                }
            }
        }
```

```
        System.out.println("Sorted array: " + Arrays.toString(array));
    }
}
```

Output:

Sorted array: [11, 12, 22, 25, 34, 64, 90]

158. IMPLEMENT SELECTION SORT ALGORITHM

```java
import java.util.Arrays;

public class SelectionSort {
    public static void main(String[] args) {
        int[] array = {64, 25, 12, 22, 11};

        for (int i = 0; i < array.length - 1; i++) {
            int minIndex = i;
            for (int j = i + 1; j < array.length; j++) {
                if (array[j] < array[minIndex]) {
                    minIndex = j;
                }
            }
            int temp = array[minIndex];
            array[minIndex] = array[i];
            array[i] = temp;
```

        }

    System.out.println("Sorted array: " + Arrays.toString(array));
  }
}

Output:

Sorted array: [11, 12, 22, 25, 64]

159. IMPLEMENT INSERTION SORT ALGORITHM

```java
import java.util.Arrays;

public class InsertionSort {
    public static void main(String[] args) {
        int[] array = {12, 11, 13, 5, 6};

        for (int i = 1; i < array.length; i++) {
            int key = array[i];
            int j = i - 1;

            while (j >= 0 && array[j] > key) {
                array[j + 1] = array[j];
                j = j - 1;
            }
            array[j + 1] = key;
        }
```

```java
        System.out.println("Sorted array: " + Arrays.toString(array));
    }
}
```

Output:

Sorted array: [5, 6, 11, 12, 13]

160. IMPLEMENT MERGE SORT ALGORITHM

```java
import java.util.Arrays;

public class MergeSort {
    public static void main(String[] args) {
        int[] array = {12, 11, 13, 5, 6, 7};
        mergeSort(array, 0, array.length - 1);
        System.out.println("Sorted array: " + Arrays.toString(array));
    }

    public static void mergeSort(int[] array, int left, int right) {
        if (left < right) {
            int mid = (left + right) / 2;
            mergeSort(array, left, mid);
            mergeSort(array, mid + 1, right);
            merge(array, left, mid, right);
```

```java
        }
    }


    public static void merge(int[] array, int left, int mid, int right) {

        int n1 = mid - left + 1;
        int n2 = right - mid;

        int[] leftArray = new int[n1];
        int[] rightArray = new int[n2];

        for (int i = 0; i < n1; i++) {
            leftArray[i] = array[left + i];
        }
        for (int i = 0; i < n2; i++) {
            rightArray[i] = array[mid + 1 + i];
        }

        int i = 0, j = 0, k = left;
```

```
while (i < n1 && j < n2) {
    if (leftArray[i] <= rightArray[j]) {
        array[k] = leftArray[i];
        i++;
    } else {
        array[k] = rightArray[j];
        j++;
    }
    k++;
}


while (i < n1) {
    array[k] = leftArray[i];
    i++;
    k++;
}


while (j < n2) {
    array[k] = rightArray[j];
```

```
            j++;
            k++;
        }
    }
}
```

Output:

Sorted array: [5, 6, 7, 11, 12, 13]

161. IMPLEMENT QUICK SORT ALGORITHM

```java
import java.util.Arrays;

public class QuickSort {
    public static void main(String[] args) {
        int[] array = {10, 7, 8, 9, 1, 5};
        quickSort(array, 0, array.length - 1);
        System.out.println("Sorted array: " + Arrays.toString(array));
    }


    public static void quickSort(int[] array, int low, int high) {
        if (low < high) {
            int pi = partition(array, low, high);
            quickSort(array, low, pi - 1);
            quickSort(array, pi + 1, high);
        }
```

}

```java
public static int partition(int[] array, int low, int high) {
    int pivot = array[high];
    int i = (low - 1);
    for (int j = low; j < high; j++) {
        if (array[j] < pivot) {
            i++;
            int temp = array[i];
            array[i] = array[j];
            array[j] = temp;
        }
    }

    int temp = array[i + 1];
    array[i + 1] = array[high];
    array[high] = temp;
```

        return i + 1;
    }
}

Output:

Sorted array: [1, 5, 7, 8, 9, 10]

162. IMPLEMENT BINARY SEARCH ALGORITHM

```java
public class BinarySearch {
    public static void main(String[] args) {
        int[] array = {2, 3, 4, 10, 40};
        int target = 10;
        int result = binarySearch(array, 0, array.length - 1, target);

        if (result == -1) {
            System.out.println("Element not present");
        } else {
            System.out.println("Element found at index: " + result);
        }
    }
```

```java
public static int binarySearch(int[] array, int left, int right, int target) {

    if (right >= left) {

        int mid = left + (right - left) / 2;

        if (array[mid] == target) {

            return mid;

        }


        if (array[mid] > target) {

            return binarySearch(array, left, mid - 1, target);

        }


        return binarySearch(array, mid + 1, right, target);

    }


    return -1;

}
```

}

Output:

Element found at index: 3

163. CHECK IF AN ARRAY IS SORTED IN ASCENDING ORDER

```java
public class CheckSortedArray {
    public static void main(String[] args) {
        int[] array = {1, 2, 3, 4, 5};
        boolean isSorted = true;

        for (int i = 1; i < array.length; i++) {
            if (array[i] < array[i - 1]) {
                isSorted = false;
                break;
            }
        }

        if (isSorted) {
            System.out.println("Array is sorted in ascending order.");
        } else {
```

```java
            System.out.println("Array is not sorted.");
        }
    }
}
```

Output:

Array is sorted in ascending order.

164. FIND THE MEDIAN OF AN ARRAY

```java
import java.util.Arrays;

public class FindMedian {
    public static void main(String[] args) {
        int[] array = {1, 3, 4, 2, 5};
        Arrays.sort(array);

        double median;
        int middle = array.length / 2;
        if (array.length % 2 == 0) {
            median = ((double)array[middle - 1] + array[middle]) / 2;
        } else {
            median = array[middle];
        }
```

```java
        System.out.println("Median: " + median);
    }
}
```

Output:

Median: 3.0

165. COUNT THE NUMBER OF VOWELS AND CONSONANTS IN A STRING

```java
public class CountVowelsConsonants {
    public static void main(String[] args) {
        String str = "hello world";
        int vowels = 0, consonants = 0;

        for (char c : str.toCharArray()) {
            if (Character.isLetter(c)) {
                c = Character.toLowerCase(c);
                if (c == 'a' || c == 'e' || c == 'i' || c == 'o' || c == 'u') {
                    vowels++;
                } else {
                    consonants++;
                }
            }
        }
    }
```

```
    System.out.println("Vowels: " + vowels);

    System.out.println("Consonants: " + consonants);

  }
}
```

Output:

Vowels: 3

Consonants: 7

166. CONVERT A DECIMAL NUMBER TO BINARY

```java
public class DecimalToBinary {
    public static void main(String[] args) {
        int num = 10;
        String binary = "";

        while (num > 0) {
            binary = (num % 2) + binary;
            num = num / 2;
        }

        System.out.println("Binary: " + binary);
    }
}
```

Output:

Binary: 1010

167. CONVERT A BINARY NUMBER TO DECIMAL

```java
public class BinaryToDecimal {
    public static void main(String[] args) {
        String binary = "1010";
        int decimal = Integer.parseInt(binary, 2);
        System.out.println("Decimal: " + decimal);
    }
}
```

Output:

Decimal: 10

168. CHECK IF A NUMBER IS PALINDROME

```java
public class PalindromeNumber {
    public static void main(String[] args) {
        int num = 121;
        int originalNum = num;
        int reversedNum = 0;

        while (num != 0) {
            int digit = num % 10;
            reversedNum = reversedNum * 10 + digit;
            num /= 10;
        }

        if (originalNum == reversedNum) {
            System.out.println(originalNum + " is a palindrome.");
        } else {
```

```
        System.out.println(originalNum + " is not a palindrome.");
    }
  }
}
```

Output:

121 is a palindrome.

169. CHECK IF A STRING IS PALINDROME

```java
public class PalindromeString {
    public static void main(String[] args) {
        String str = "madam";
        String reversedStr = new StringBuilder(str).reverse().toString();

        if (str.equals(reversedStr)) {
            System.out.println(str + " is a palindrome.");
        } else {
            System.out.println(str + " is not a palindrome.");
        }
    }
}
```

Output:

madam is a palindrome.

170. FIND THE LARGEST ELEMENT IN AN ARRAY

```java
public class LargestElement {
    public static void main(String[] args) {
        int[] array = {10, 20, 30, 5, 15};
        int max = array[0];

        for (int i = 1; i < array.length; i++) {
            if (array[i] > max) {
                max = array[i];
            }
        }
        System.out.println("Largest element: " + max);
    }
}
```

Output:

Largest element: 30

171. FIND THE SMALLEST ELEMENT IN AN ARRAY

```java
public class SmallestElement {
    public static void main(String[] args) {
        int[] array = {10, 20, 30, 5, 15};
        int min = array[0];

        for (int i = 1; i < array.length; i++) {
            if (array[i] < min) {
                min = array[i];
            }
        }
        System.out.println("Smallest element: " + min);
    }
}
```

Output:

Smallest element: 5

172. REVERSE AN ARRAY

```java
import java.util.Arrays;
public class ReverseArray {
    public static void main(String[] args) {
        int[] array = {1, 2, 3, 4, 5};
        int n = array.length;

        for (int i = 0; i < n / 2; i++) {
            int temp = array[i];
            array[i] = array[n - i - 1];
            array[n - i - 1] = temp;
        }
        System.out.println("Reversed array: " + Arrays.toString(array));
    }
}
```

Output:

Reversed array: [5, 4, 3, 2, 1]

173. SUM OF DIAGONALS IN A MATRIX

```java
public class SumOfDiagonals {
    public static void main(String[] args) {
        int[][] matrix = {
            {1, 2, 3},
            {4, 5, 6},
            {7, 8, 9}
        };
        int primaryDiagonalSum = 0;
        int secondaryDiagonalSum = 0;

        for (int i = 0; i < matrix.length; i++) {
            primaryDiagonalSum += matrix[i][i];
            secondaryDiagonalSum += matrix[i][matrix.length - i - 1];
        }
```

```java
        System.out.println("Primary Diagonal Sum: " + primaryDiagonalSum);

        System.out.println("Secondary Diagonal Sum: " + secondaryDiagonalSum);
    }
}
```

Output:

Primary Diagonal Sum: 15

Secondary Diagonal Sum: 15

174. FIND THE SECOND LARGEST ELEMENT IN AN ARRAY

```java
public class SecondLargestElement {

    public static void main(String[] args) {

        int[] array = {10, 20, 30, 5, 15};

        int firstLargest = Integer.MIN_VALUE;

        int secondLargest = Integer.MIN_VALUE;


        for (int i = 0; i < array.length; i++) {

            if (array[i] > firstLargest) {

                secondLargest = firstLargest;

                firstLargest = array[i];

            } else if (array[i] > secondLargest && array[i] != firstLargest) {

                secondLargest = array[i];

            }

        }
```

```java
        System.out.println("Second largest element: " + secondLargest);
    }
}
```

Output:

Second largest element: 20

175. FIND THE FREQUENCY OF EACH ELEMENT IN AN ARRAY

```java
import java.util.HashMap;
import java.util.Map;
public class FrequencyOfElements {
    public static void main(String[] args) {
        int[] array = {1, 2, 2, 3, 3, 3, 4};
        Map<Integer, Integer> frequencyMap = new HashMap<>();

        for (int num : array) {
            frequencyMap.put(num, frequencyMap.getOrDefault(num, 0) + 1);
        }
        System.out.println("Frequency of elements: " + frequencyMap); }
}
```

Output:

Frequency of elements: {1=1, 2=2, 3=3, 4=1}

176. CONVERT A STRING TO UPPERCASE WITHOUT USING BUILT-IN FUNCTION

```java
public class ToUppercase {
    public static void main(String[] args) {
        String str = "hello world";
        StringBuilder upperStr = new StringBuilder();
        for (char c : str.toCharArray()) {
            if (c >= 'a' && c <= 'z') {
                c = (char)(c - 'a' + 'A');
            }
            upperStr.append(c);
        }
        System.out.println("Uppercase: " + upperStr);   }
}
```

Output:

Uppercase: HELLO WORLD

177. CONVERT A STRING TO LOWERCASE WITHOUT USING BUILT-IN FUNCTION

```java
public class ToLowercase {
    public static void main(String[] args) {
        String str = "HELLO WORLD";
        StringBuilder lowerStr = new StringBuilder();
        for (char c : str.toCharArray()) {
            if (c >= 'A' && c <= 'Z') {
                c = (char)(c - 'A' + 'a');
            }
            lowerStr.append(c);
        }
        System.out.println("Lowercase: " + lowerStr);
    }
}
```

Output:

Lowercase: hello world

178. FIND THE MAXIMUM AND MINIMUM ELEMENTS IN AN ARRAY

```java
public class MaxMinArray {
    public static void main(String[] args) {
        int[] array = {1, 2, 3, 4, 5};
        int max = array[0];
        int min = array[0];

        for (int i = 1; i < array.length; i++) {
            if (array[i] > max) {
                max = array[i];
            }
            if (array[i] < min) {
                min = array[i];
            }
        }
```

181. IMPLEMENT A SIMPLE CALCULATOR

```java
import java.util.Scanner;

public class SimpleCalculator {

    public static void main(String[] args) {

        Scanner scanner = new Scanner(System.in);

        System.out.println("Enter first number: ");

        double num1 = scanner.nextDouble();

        System.out.println("Enter second number: ");

        double num2 = scanner.nextDouble();

        System.out.println("Choose an operation (+, -, *, /): ");

        char operation = scanner.next().charAt(0);

        double result;

        switch (operation) {
```

```java
        case '+':
            result = num1 + num2;
            break;
        case '-':
            result = num1 - num2;
            break;
        case '*':
            result = num1 * num2;
            break;
        case '/':
            result = num1 / num2;
            break;
        default:
            System.out.println("Invalid operation");
            return;
    }
    System.out.println("Result: " + result);
}
```

}

Output :

Enter first number: 10 Enter second number: 5 Choose an operation (+, -, *, /): + Result: 15.0

182. PRINT FIBONACCI SERIES UP TO N TERMS

```java
public class FibonacciSeries {
    public static void main(String[] args) {
        int n = 10;
        int a = 0, b = 1;
        System.out.print("Fibonacci Series up to " + n + " terms: ");
        for (int i = 0; i < n; i++) {
            System.out.print(a + " ");
            int next = a + b;
            a = b;
            b = next;
        }
    }
}
```

Output:

Fibonacci Series up to 10 terms: 0 1 1 2 3 5 8 13 21 34

183. COUNT THE NUMBER OF WORDS IN A STRING

```java
public class CountWords {
    public static void main(String[] args) {
        String str = "This is a simple sentence.";
        String[] words = str.split("\\s+");
        System.out.println("Number of words: " + words.length);
    }
}
```

Output:

Number of words: 5

184. FIND THE SUM OF ALL ODD NUMBERS FROM 1 TO N

```java
public class SumOfOdds {
    public static void main(String[] args) {
        int n = 10;
        int sum = 0;

        for (int i = 1; i <= n; i += 2) {
            sum += i;
        }

        System.out.println("Sum of odd numbers from 1 to " + n + " is: " + sum);
    }
}
```

Output:

Sum of odd numbers from 1 to 10 is: 25

185. FIND THE SUM OF ALL EVEN NUMBERS FROM 1 TO N

```java
public class SumOfEvens {
    public static void main(String[] args) {
        int n = 10;
        int sum = 0;

        for (int i = 2; i <= n; i += 2) {
            sum += i;
        }

        System.out.println("Sum of even numbers from 1 to " + n + " is: " + sum);
    }
}
```

Output:

Sum of even numbers from 1 to 10 is: 30

186. COUNT THE NUMBER OF VOWELS IN A STRING

```java
public class CountVowelsInString {
    public static void main(String[] args) {
        String str = "Hello World";
        int vowelCount = 0;
        for (char c : str.toLowerCase().toCharArray()) {
            if (c == 'a' || c == 'e' || c == 'i' || c == 'o' || c == 'u') {
                vowelCount++;
            }
        }
        System.out.println("Number of vowels: " + vowelCount);
    }
}
```

Output:

Number of vowels: 3

187. GENERATE A RANDOM NUMBER BETWEEN 1 AND 100

```java
import java.util.Random;

public class RandomNumber {
    public static void main(String[] args) {
        Random rand = new Random();
        int randomNumber = rand.nextInt(100) + 1; // Generates a number between 1 and 100
        System.out.println("Random number between 1 and 100: " + randomNumber);
    }
}
```

Output (example):

Random number between 1 and 100: 42

188. COUNT THE NUMBER OF DIGITS IN AN INTEGER

```java
public class CountDigits {
    public static void main(String[] args) {
        int num = 123456;
        int count = 0;

        while (num != 0) {
            num /= 10;
            count++;
        }

        System.out.println("Number of digits: " + count);
    }
}
```

Output:

Number of digits: 6

189. PRINT A RIGHT-ANGLE TRIANGLE PATTERN

```java
public class RightAngleTriangle {
    public static void main(String[] args) {
        int rows = 5;

        for (int i = 1; i <= rows; i++) {
            for (int j = 1; j <= i; j++) {
                System.out.print("* ");
            }
            System.out.println();
        }
    }
}
```

Output:

```
*
* *
* * *
* * * *
* * * * *
```

190. PRINT A PYRAMID PATTERN

```java
public class PyramidPattern {
    public static void main(String[] args) {
        int rows = 5;

        for (int i = 1; i <= rows; i++) {
            for (int j = rows; j > i; j--) {
                System.out.print(" ");
            }
            for (int k = 1; k <= (2 * i - 1); k++) {
                System.out.print("*");
            }
            System.out.println();
        }
    }
}
```

Output:

```
    *
   ***
  *****
 *******
*********
```

191. PRINT A DIAMOND PATTERN

```java
public class DiamondPattern {
    public static void main(String[] args) {
        int n = 5;

        // Upper half
        for (int i = 1; i <= n; i++) {
            for (int j = n; j > i; j--) {
                System.out.print(" ");
            }
            for (int k = 1; k <= (2 * i - 1); k++) {
                System.out.print("*");
            }
            System.out.println();
        }

        // Lower half
```

```java
        for (int i = n - 1; i >= 1; i--) {
            for (int j = n; j > i; j--) {
                System.out.print(" ");
            }
            for (int k = 1; k <= (2 * i - 1); k++) {
                System.out.print("*");
            }
            System.out.println();
        }
    }
}
```

Output:

```
    *
   ***
  *****
 *******
*********
 *******
  *****
   ***
    *
```

192. PRINT THE MULTIPLICATION TABLE OF A GIVEN NUMBER

```java
public class MultiplicationTable {
    public static void main(String[] args) {
        int number = 5;

        for (int i = 1; i <= 10; i++) {
            System.out.println(number + " x " + i + " = " + (number * i));
        }
    }
}
```

Output:

5 x 1 = 5

5 x 2 = 10

5 x 3 = 15

5 x 4 = 20

5 x 5 = 25

5 x 6 = 30

5 x 7 = 35

5 x 8 = 40

5 x 9 = 45

5 x 10 = 50

193. CHECK IF A NUMBER IS PRIME

```java
public class PrimeCheck {
    public static void main(String[] args) {
        int num = 29;
        boolean isPrime = true;

        if (num <= 1) {
            isPrime = false;
        } else {
            for (int i = 2; i <= Math.sqrt(num); i++) {
                if (num % i == 0) {
                    isPrime = false;
                    break;
                }
            }
        }
```

```java
        if (isPrime) {
            System.out.println(num + " is a prime number.");
        } else {
            System.out.println(num + " is not a prime number.");
        }
    }
}
```

Output:

29 is a prime number.

194. CALCULATE FACTORIAL OF A NUMBER

```java
public class Factorial {
    public static void main(String[] args) {
        int num = 5;
        long factorial = 1;

        for (int i = 1; i <= num; i++) {
            factorial *= i;
        }

        System.out.println("Factorial of " + num + " is: " + factorial);
    }
}
```

Output:

Factorial of 5 is: 120

195. FIND THE SUM OF NATURAL NUMBERS UP TO N

```java
public class SumOfNaturalNumbers {
    public static void main(String[] args) {
        int n = 10;
        int sum = n * (n + 1) / 2;


        System.out.println("Sum of natural numbers up to " + n + " is: " + sum);
    }
}
```

Output:

Sum of natural numbers up to 10 is: 55

196. PRINT THE FIBONACCI SERIES USING RECURSION

```java
public class FibonacciRecursion {
    public static void main(String[] args) {
        int n = 10;
        for (int i = 0; i < n; i++) {
            System.out.print(fibonacci(i) + " ");
        }
    }
    public static int fibonacci(int n) {
        if (n <= 1) {
            return n;
        }
        return fibonacci(n - 1) + fibonacci(n - 2);
    }
}
```

Output:

0 1 1 2 3 5 8 13 21 34

197. FIND THE SUM OF DIGITS OF A NUMBER

```java
public class SumOfDigits {
    public static void main(String[] args) {
        int num = 12345;
        int sum = 0;

        while (num != 0) {
            sum += num % 10;
            num /= 10;
        }

        System.out.println("Sum of digits: " + sum);
    }
}
```

Output:

Sum of digits: 15

198. CHECK IF A NUMBER IS EVEN OR ODD

```java
public class EvenOddCheck {
    public static void main(String[] args) {
        int num = 7;

        if (num % 2 == 0) {
            System.out.println(num + " is even.");
        } else {
            System.out.println(num + " is odd.");
        }
    }
}
```

Output:

7 is odd.

199. COUNT THE NUMBER OF SPACES IN A STRING

```java
public class CountSpaces {
    public static void main(String[] args) {
        String str = "Count the number of spaces";
        int spaceCount = 0;

        for (char c : str.toCharArray()) {
            if (c == ' ') {
                spaceCount++;
            }
        }
        System.out.println("Number of spaces: " + spaceCount);
    }
}
```

Output:

Number of spaces: 4

200. FIND THE COMMON ELEMENTS BETWEEN TWO ARRAYS

```java
import java.util.HashSet;
import java.util.Set;

public class CommonElements {
    public static void main(String[] args) {
        int[] array1 = {1, 2, 3, 4, 5};
        int[] array2 = {4, 5, 6, 7, 8};

        Set<Integer> set1 = new HashSet<>();
        for (int num : array1) {
            set1.add(num);
        }

        System.out.print("Common elements: ");
        for (int num : array2) {
```

```java
            if (set1.contains(num)) {
                System.out.print(num + " ");
            }
        }
    }
}
```

Output:

Common elements: 4 5

201. CONVERT BINARY TO DECIMAL

```java
public class BinaryToDecimal {
    public static void main(String[] args) {
        String binary = "1101";
        int decimal = Integer.parseInt(binary, 2);
        System.out.println("Binary " + binary + " in decimal is: " + decimal);
    }
}
```

Output:

Binary 1101 in decimal is: 13

202. CONVERT DECIMAL TO BINARY

```java
public class DecimalToBinary {
    public static void main(String[] args) {
        int decimal = 13;
        String binary = Integer.toBinaryString(decimal);
        System.out.println("Decimal " + decimal + " in binary is: " + binary);
    }
}
```

Output:

Decimal 13 in binary is: 1101

203. SWAP TWO NUMBERS WITHOUT USING A TEMPORARY VARIABLE

```java
public class SwapWithoutTemp {
    public static void main(String[] args) {
        int a = 5;
        int b = 10;

        a = a + b;
        b = a - b;
        a = a - b;

        System.out.println("After swapping: a = " + a + ", b = " + b);
    }
}
```

Output:

After swapping: a = 10, b = 5

204. CHECK IF A NUMBER IS ARMSTRONG

```java
public class ArmstrongNumber {
    public static void main(String[] args) {
        int num = 153;
        int originalNum = num;
        int result = 0;

        while (originalNum != 0) {
            int digit = originalNum % 10;
            result += Math.pow(digit, 3);
            originalNum /= 10;
        }

        if (result == num) {
            System.out.println(num + " is an Armstrong number.");
        } else {
```

```
            System.out.println(num + " is not an Armstrong number.");
        }
    }
}
```

Output:

153 is an Armstrong number.

205. CHECK IF A NUMBER IS PERFECT

```java
public class PerfectNumber {
    public static void main(String[] args) {
        int num = 28;
        int sum = 0;

        for (int i = 1; i < num; i++) {
            if (num % i == 0) {
                sum += i;
            }
        }

        if (sum == num) {
            System.out.println(num + " is a perfect number.");
        } else {
            System.out.println(num + " is not a perfect number.");
```

        }
    }
}

Output:

28 is a perfect number.

206. CHECK IF A STRING IS A PALINDROME (IGNORING CASE)

```java
public class PalindromeIgnoreCase {
    public static void main(String[] args) {
        String str = "Madam";
        String lowerStr = str.toLowerCase();
        String reversedStr = new StringBuilder(lowerStr).reverse().toString();
        if (lowerStr.equals(reversedStr)) {
            System.out.println(str + " is a palindrome.");
        } else {
            System.out.println(str + " is not a palindrome.");
        }
    }
}
```

Output:

Madam is a palindrome.

207. FIND THE SUM OF ALL PRIME NUMBERS UP TO N

```java
public class SumOfPrimes {
    public static void main(String[] args) {
        int n = 10;
        int sum = 0;

        for (int i = 2; i <= n; i++) {
            if (isPrime(i)) {
                sum += i;
            }
        }

        System.out.println("Sum of prime numbers up to " + n + " is: " + sum);
    }

    public static boolean isPrime(int num) {
        if (num <= 1) {
```

```
            return false;
        }
        for (int i = 2; i <= Math.sqrt(num); i++) {
            if (num % i == 0) {
                return false;
            }
        }
        return true;
    }
}
```

Output:

Sum of prime numbers up to 10 is: 17

208. FIND THE GCD OF TWO NUMBERS

```java
public class GCD {
    public static void main(String[] args) {
        int num1 = 56;
        int num2 = 98;
        int gcd = 1;
        for (int i = 1; i <= num1 && i <= num2; i++) {
            if (num1 % i == 0 && num2 % i == 0) {
                gcd = i;
            }
        }
        System.out.println("GCD of " + num1 + " and " + num2 + " is: " + gcd);
    }
}
```

Output:

GCD of 56 and 98 is: 14

209. FIND THE LCM OF TWO NUMBERS

```java
public class LCM {
    public static void main(String[] args) {
        int num1 = 72;
        int num2 = 120;
        int lcm = (num1 > num2) ? num1 : num2;
        while (true) {
            if (lcm % num1 == 0 && lcm % num2 == 0) {
                System.out.println("LCM of " + num1 + " and " + num2 + " is: " + lcm);
                break;
            }
            lcm++; }
    }
}
```

Output:

LCM of 72 and 120 is: 360

210. CONVERT CELSIUS TO FAHRENHEIT

```java
public class CelsiusToFahrenheit {
    public static void main(String[] args) {
        double celsius = 25.0;
        double fahrenheit = (celsius * 9/5) + 32;
        System.out.println(celsius + "°C is equal to " + fahrenheit + "°F");
    }
}
```

Output:

25.0°C is equal to 77.0°F

211. CONVERT FAHRENHEIT TO CELSIUS

```java
public class FahrenheitToCelsius {
    public static void main(String[] args) {
        double fahrenheit = 77.0;
        double celsius = (fahrenheit - 32) * 5/9;
        System.out.println(fahrenheit + "°F is equal to " + celsius + "°C");
    }
}
```

Output:

77.0°F is equal to 25.0°C

212. COUNT THE NUMBER OF CONSONANTS IN A STRING

```java
public class CountConsonants {
    public static void main(String[] args) {
        String str = "Hello World";
        int consonantCount = 0;

        for (char c : str.toLowerCase().toCharArray()) {
            if ((c >= 'a' && c <= 'z') && !(c == 'a' || c == 'e' || c == 'i' || c == 'o' || c == 'u')) {
                consonantCount++;
            }
        }
        System.out.println("Number of consonants: " + consonantCount);
    }
}
```

Output:

Number of consonants: 7

213. FIND THE FACTORIAL OF A NUMBER USING RECURSION

```java
public class FactorialRecursion {
    public static void main(String[] args) {
        int num = 5;
        System.out.println("Factorial of " + num + " is: " + factorial(num));
    }


    public static int factorial(int n) {
        if (n == 0) {
            return 1;
        } else {
            return n * factorial(n - 1);
        }
    }
}
```

Output:

Factorial of 5 is: 120

214. REVERSE A NUMBER

```java
public class ReverseNumber {
    public static void main(String[] args) {
        int num = 12345;
        int reversed = 0;

        while (num != 0) {
            int digit = num % 10;
            reversed = reversed * 10 + digit;
            num /= 10;
        }

        System.out.println("Reversed number: " + reversed);
    }
}
```

Output:

Reversed number: 54321

215. FIND THE FIRST NON-REPEATED CHARACTER IN A STRING

```java
import java.util.LinkedHashMap;
import java.util.Map;


public class FirstNonRepeatedCharacter {
    public static void main(String[] args) {
        String str = "swiss";
        Map<Character, Integer> charCountMap = new LinkedHashMap<>();


        for (char c : str.toCharArray()) {
            charCountMap.put(c, charCountMap.getOrDefault(c, 0) + 1);
        }


        for (Map.Entry<Character, Integer> entry : charCountMap.entrySet()) {
```

```java
            if (entry.getValue() == 1) {
                System.out.println("First non-repeated character: " + entry.getKey());
                break;
            }
        }
    }
}
```

Output:

First non-repeated character: w

216. PRINT THE FIBONACCI SERIES USING A WHILE LOOP

```java
public class FibonacciWhileLoop {
    public static void main(String[] args) {
        int n = 10;
        int a = 0, b = 1;
        int count = 0;

        System.out.print("Fibonacci Series up to " + n + " terms: ");
        while (count < n) {
            System.out.print(a + " ");
            int next = a + b;
            a = b;
            b = next;
            count++;
        }
    }
```

}

Output:

Fibonacci Series up to 10 terms: 0 1 1 2 3 5 8 13 21 34

217. GENERATE THE FIRST N PRIME NUMBERS

```java
public class FirstNPrimes {
    public static void main(String[] args) {
        int n = 5;
        int count = 0;
        int num = 2;

        while (count < n) {
            if (isPrime(num)) {
                System.out.print(num + " ");
                count++;
            }
            num++;
        }
    }

    public static boolean isPrime(int num) {
```

```
        if (num <= 1) {
            return false;
        }
        for (int i = 2; i <= Math.sqrt(num); i++) {
            if (num % i == 0) {
                return false;
            }
        }
        return true;
    }
}
```

Output:

2 3 5 7 11

218. FIND THE LARGEST ELEMENT IN AN ARRAY

```java
public class LargestElementInArray {
    public static void main(String[] args) {
        int[] array = {10, 25, 5, 50, 40};
        int largest = array[0];

        for (int num : array) {
            if (num > largest) {
                largest = num;
            }
        }
        System.out.println("Largest element in the array: " + largest);
    }
}
```

Output:

Largest element in the array: 50

219. FIND THE SMALLEST ELEMENT IN AN ARRAY

```java
public class SmallestElementInArray {
    public static void main(String[] args) {
        int[] array = {10, 25, 5, 50, 40};
        int smallest = array[0];

        for (int num : array) {
            if (num < smallest) {
                smallest = num;
            }
        }
        System.out.println("Smallest element in the array: " + smallest);
    }
}
```

Output:

Smallest element in the array: 5

220. CHECK IF TWO STRINGS ARE ANAGRAMS

```java
import java.util.Arrays;

public class AnagramCheck {
    public static void main(String[] args) {
        String str1 = "listen";
        String str2 = "silent";

        char[] arr1 = str1.toCharArray();
        char[] arr2 = str2.toCharArray();

        Arrays.sort(arr1);
        Arrays.sort(arr2);

        if (Arrays.equals(arr1, arr2)) {
            System.out.println(str1 + " and " + str2 + " are anagrams.");
```

```java
        } else {
            System.out.println(str1 + " and " + str2 + " are not anagrams.");
        }
    }
}
```

Output:

listen and silent are anagrams.

221. CALCULATE THE POWER OF A NUMBER USING A LOOP

```java
public class PowerOfNumber {
    public static void main(String[] args) {
        int base = 2;
        int exponent = 5;
        int result = 1;

        for (int i = 0; i < exponent; i++) {
            result *= base;
        }
        System.out.println(base + " raised to the power of " + exponent + " is: " + result);
    }
}
```

Output:

2 raised to the power of 5 is: 32

222. FIND THE SECOND LARGEST ELEMENT IN AN ARRAY

```java
public class SecondLargestInArray {
    public static void main(String[] args) {
        int[] array = {10, 25, 5, 50, 40};
        int largest = Integer.MIN_VALUE;
        int secondLargest = Integer.MIN_VALUE;

        for (int num : array) {
            if (num > largest) {
                secondLargest = largest;
                largest = num;
            } else if (num > secondLargest && num != largest) {
                secondLargest = num;
            }
        }
```

```java
        System.out.println("Second largest element in the array: " + secondLargest);
    }
}
```

Output:

Second largest element in the array: 40

223. FIND THE SECOND SMALLEST ELEMENT IN AN ARRAY

```java
public class SecondSmallestInArray {
    public static void main(String[] args) {
        int[] array = {10, 25, 5, 50, 40};
        int smallest = Integer.MAX_VALUE;
        int secondSmallest = Integer.MAX_VALUE;

        for (int num : array) {
            if (num < smallest) {
                secondSmallest = smallest;
                smallest = num;
            } else if (num < secondSmallest && num != smallest) {
                secondSmallest = num;
            }
        }
```

```
        System.out.println("Second smallest
element in the array: " + secondSmallest);

    }
}
```

Output:

Second smallest element in the array: 10

224. CALCULATE THE AVERAGE OF ELEMENTS IN AN ARRAY

```java
public class AverageOfArray {
    public static void main(String[] args) {
        int[] array = {10, 25, 5, 50, 40};
        int sum = 0;

        for (int num : array) {
            sum += num;
        }
        double average = sum / (double) array.length;
        System.out.println("Average of elements in the array: " + average);
    }
}
```

Output:

Average of elements in the array: 26.0

225. FIND THE MAXIMUM AND MINIMUM VALUES IN AN ARRAY

```java
public class MaxMinArray {
    public static void main(String[] args) {
        int[] array = {10, 25, 5, 50, 40};
        int max = array[0];
        int min = array[0];

        for (int num : array) {
            if (num > max) {
                max = num;
            }
            if (num < min) {
                min = num;
            }
        }

        System.out.println("Maximum value: " + max);
```

```
      System.out.println("Minimum value: " + min);
   }
}
```

Output:

Maximum value: 50

Minimum value: 5

226. FIND THE SUM OF EACH ROW IN A 2D ARRAY

```java
public class SumOfRows2DArray {
    public static void main(String[] args) {
        int[][] array = {
            {1, 2, 3},
            {4, 5, 6},
            {7, 8, 9}
        };

        for (int i = 0; i < array.length; i++) {
            int sum = 0;
            for (int j = 0; j < array[i].length; j++) {
                sum += array[i][j];
            }
            System.out.println("Sum of row " + (i+1) + ": " + sum);
        }
```

}
}

Output:

Sum of row 1: 6

Sum of row 2: 15

Sum of row 3: 24

227. FIND THE SUM OF EACH COLUMN IN A 2D ARRAY

```java
public class SumOfColumns2DArray {
    public static void main(String[] args) {
        int[][] array = {
            {1, 2, 3},
            {4, 5, 6},
            {7, 8, 9}
        };

        for (int j = 0; j < array[0].length; j++) {
            int sum = 0;
            for (int i = 0; i < array.length; i++) {
                sum += array[i][j];
            }
            System.out.println("Sum of column " + (j+1) + ": " + sum);
        }
```

        }
}

Output:

Sum of column 1: 12

Sum of column 2: 15

Sum of column 3: 18

228. REVERSE THE ELEMENTS OF AN ARRAY

```java
import java.util.Arrays;
public class ReverseArray {
    public static void main(String[] args) {
        int[] array = {10, 25, 5, 50, 40};
        int n = array.length;
        for (int i = 0; i < n / 2; i++) {
            int temp = array[i];
            array[i] = array[n - 1 - i];
            array[n - 1 - i] = temp;
        }
        System.out.println("Reversed array: " + Arrays.toString(array));
    }
}
```

Output:

Reversed array: [40, 50, 5, 25, 10]

229. MERGE TWO ARRAYS INTO A SINGLE ARRAY

```java
import java.util.Arrays;
public class MergeArrays {
    public static void main(String[] args) {
        int[] array1 = {1, 2, 3};
        int[] array2 = {4, 5, 6};
        int[] mergedArray = new int[array1.length + array2.length];
        System.arraycopy(array1, 0, mergedArray, 0, array1.length);
        System.arraycopy(array2, 0, mergedArray, array1.length, array2.length);
        System.out.println("Merged array: " + Arrays.toString(mergedArray));
    }
}
```

Output:

Merged array: [1, 2, 3, 4, 5, 6]

230. ROTATE AN ARRAY TO THE LEFT BY ONE POSITION

```java
import java.util.Arrays;
public class RotateLeft {
    public static void main(String[] args) {
        int[] array = {1, 2, 3, 4, 5};

        int first = array[0];
        for (int i = 0; i < array.length - 1; i++) {
            array[i] = array[i + 1];
        }
        array[array.length - 1] = first;

        System.out.println("Array after left rotation: " + Arrays.toString(array));
    }
}
```

Output:

Array after left rotation: [2, 3, 4, 5, 1]

231. ROTATE AN ARRAY TO THE RIGHT BY ONE POSITION

```java
import java.util.Arrays;
public class RotateRight {
    public static void main(String[] args) {
        int[] array = {1, 2, 3, 4, 5};

        int last = array[array.length - 1];
        for (int i = array.length - 1; i > 0; i--) {
            array[i] = array[i - 1];
        }
        array[0] = last;

        System.out.println("Array after right rotation: " + Arrays.toString(array));
    }
}
```

Output:

Array after right rotation: [5, 1, 2, 3, 4]

232. COUNT THE NUMBER OF WORDS IN A STRING

```java
public class CountWords {
    public static void main(String[] args) {
        String str = "This is a sample string";
        String[] words = str.split("\\s+");
        System.out.println("Number of words: " + words.length);
    }
}
```

Output:

Number of words: 5

233. CONVERT A CHARACTER TO ITS ASCII VALUE

```java
public class CharToASCII {
    public static void main(String[] args) {
        char c = 'A';
        int asciiValue = (int) c;
        System.out.println("ASCII value of " + c + " is: " + asciiValue);
    }
}
```

Output:

ASCII value of A is: 65

234. FIND THE LENGTH OF A STRING WITHOUT USING LENGTH() METHOD

```java
public class StringLength {
    public static void main(String[] args) {
        String str = "Hello, World!";
        int length = 0;

        for (char c : str.toCharArray()) {
            length++;
        }

        System.out.println("Length of the string: " + length);
    }
}
```

Output:

Length of the string: 13

235. FIND THE SUM OF THE ELEMENTS IN A 2D ARRAY

```java
public class Sum2DArray {
    public static void main(String[] args) {
        int[][] array = {
            {1, 2, 3},
            {4, 5, 6},
            {7, 8, 9}
        };
        int sum = 0;

        for (int[] row : array) {
            for (int num : row) {
                sum += num;
            }
        }
```

        System.out.println("Sum of all elements in 2D array: " + sum);

   }
}

Output:

Sum of all elements in 2D array: 45

236. TRANSPOSE A 2D MATRIX

```java
import java.util.Arrays;

public class TransposeMatrix {
    public static void main(String[] args) {
        int[][] matrix = {
            {1, 2, 3},
            {4, 5, 6},
            {7, 8, 9}
        };

        int[][] transpose = new int[matrix[0].length][matrix.length];

        for (int i = 0; i < matrix.length; i++) {
            for (int j = 0; j < matrix[0].length; j++) {
                transpose[j][i] = matrix[i][j];
```

```java
            }
        }

        System.out.println("Original matrix:");
        for (int[] row : matrix) {
            System.out.println(Arrays.toString(row));
        }

        System.out.println("Transposed matrix:");
        for (int[] row : transpose) {
            System.out.println(Arrays.toString(row));
        }
    }
}
```

Output:

Original matrix:

[1, 2, 3]

[4, 5, 6]

[7, 8, 9]

Transposed matrix:

[1, 4, 7]

[2, 5, 8]

[3, 6, 9]

237. MULTIPLY TWO MATRICES

```java
import java.util.Arrays;

public class MultiplyMatrices {
    public static void main(String[] args) {
        int[][] matrix1 = {
            {1, 2, 3},
            {4, 5, 6}
        };
        int[][] matrix2 = {
            {7, 8},
            {9, 10},
            {11, 12}
        };
        int[][] result = new int[matrix1.length][matrix2[0].length];
        for (int i = 0; i < matrix1.length; i++) {
            for (int j = 0; j < matrix2[0].length; j++) {
```

```java
            for (int k = 0; k < matrix2.length; k++) {
                result[i][j] += matrix1[i][k] * matrix2[k][j];
            }
        }
    }
    System.out.println("Resultant matrix:");
    for (int[] row : result) {
        System.out.println(Arrays.toString(row));
    }
  }
}
```

Output:

Resultant matrix:

[58, 64]

[139, 154]

238. COUNT THE NUMBER OF VOWELS IN A STRING

```java
public class VowelCount {

    public static void main(String[] args) {

        String str = "This is a sample string";

        int vowelCount = 0;

        for (char c : str.toLowerCase().toCharArray()) {

            if (c == 'a' || c == 'e' || c == 'i' || c == 'o' || c == 'u') {

                vowelCount++;

            }
        }


        System.out.println("Number of vowels: " + vowelCount);

    }
}
```

Output:

Number of vowels: 6

239. COUNT THE NUMBER OF CONSONANTS IN A STRING

```java
public class ConsonantCount {
    public static void main(String[] args) {
        String str = "This is a sample string";
        int consonantCount = 0;

        for (char c : str.toLowerCase().toCharArray()) {
            if ((c >= 'a' && c <= 'z') && !(c == 'a' || c == 'e' || c == 'i' || c == 'o' || c == 'u')) {
                consonantCount++;
            }
        }
        System.out.println("Number of consonants: " + consonantCount);
    }
}
```

Output:

Number of consonants: 12

240. FIND THE SUM OF EVEN AND ODD NUMBERS IN AN ARRAY SEPARATELY

```java
public class SumEvenOddArray {
    public static void main(String[] args) {
        int[] array = {1, 2, 3, 4, 5, 6};
        int sumEven = 0;
        int sumOdd = 0;

        for (int num : array) {
            if (num % 2 == 0) {
                sumEven += num;
            } else {
                sumOdd += num;
            }
        }

        System.out.println("Sum of even numbers: " + sumEven);
```

```java
        System.out.println("Sum of odd numbers: " + sumOdd);
    }
}
```

Output:

Sum of even numbers: 12

Sum of odd numbers: 9

241. FIND THE FACTORIAL OF A NUMBER USING RECURSION

```java
public class FactorialRecursion {
    public static void main(String[] args) {
        int n = 5;
        int result = factorial(n);
        System.out.println("Factorial of " + n + " is: " + result);
    }
    public static int factorial(int n) {
        if (n == 0) {
            return 1;
        }
        return n * factorial(n - 1);
    }
}
```

Output:

Factorial of 5 is: 120

242. FIND THE GREATEST COMMON DIVISOR (GCD) USING RECURSION

```java
public class GCDRecursion {
    public static void main(String[] args) {
        int a = 54;
        int b = 24;
        int gcd = gcd(a, b);
        System.out.println("GCD of " + a + " and " + b + " is: " + gcd);
    }
    public static int gcd(int a, int b) {
        if (b == 0) {
            return a;
        }
        return gcd(b, a % b);
    }
}
```

Output:

GCD of 54 and 24 is: 6

243. FIND THE LEAST COMMON MULTIPLE (LCM) USING GCD

```java
public class LCMUsingGCD {
    public static void main(String[] args) {
        int a = 54;
        int b = 24;
        int lcm = (a * b) / gcd(a, b);
        System.out.println("LCM of " + a + " and " + b + " is: " + lcm);
    }
    public static int gcd(int a, int b) {
        if (b == 0) {
            return a;
        }
        return gcd(b, a % b);
    }
}
```

Output:

LCM of 54 and 24 is: 216

244. CALCULATE THE POWER OF A NUMBER USING RECURSION

```java
public class PowerRecursion {
    public static void main(String[] args) {
        int base = 2;
        int exponent = 5;
        int result = power(base, exponent);
        System.out.println(base + " raised to the power of " + exponent + " is: " + result);
    }
    public static int power(int base, int exponent) {
        if (exponent == 0) {
            return 1;
        }
        return base * power(base, exponent - 1);
    }
}
```

Output:

2 raised to the power of 5 is: 32

245. PRINT FIBONACCI SERIES USING RECURSION

```java
public class FibonacciRecursion {
    public static void main(String[] args) {
        int n = 10;
        System.out.print("Fibonacci Series up to " + n + " terms: ");
        for (int i = 0; i < n; i++) {
            System.out.print(fibonacci(i) + " ");
        }
    }


    public static int fibonacci(int n) {
        if (n <= 1) {
            return n;
        }
        return fibonacci(n - 1) + fibonacci(n - 2);
    }
}
```

Output:

Fibonacci Series up to 10 terms: 0 1 1 2 3 5 8 13 21 34

246. REVERSE A STRING USING RECURSION

```java
public class ReverseStringRecursion {
    public static void main(String[] args) {
        String str = "Hello";
        String reversedStr = reverse(str);
        System.out.println("Reversed string: " + reversedStr);
    }
    public static String reverse(String str) {
        if (str.isEmpty()) {
            return str;
        }
        return reverse(str.substring(1)) + str.charAt(0);
    }
}
```

Output:

Reversed string: olleH

247. CHECK IF A STRING IS A PALINDROME USING RECURSION

```java
public class PalindromeRecursion {
    public static void main(String[] args) {
        String str = "madam";
        boolean isPalindrome = isPalindrome(str);
        System.out.println(str + " is a palindrome: " + isPalindrome);
    }
    public static boolean isPalindrome(String str) {
        if (str.length() == 0 || str.length() == 1) {
            return true;
        }
        if (str.charAt(0) == str.charAt(str.length() - 1)) {
            return isPalindrome(str.substring(1, str.length() - 1));
```

```
        }
        return false;
    }
}
```

Output:

madam is a palindrome: true

248. CHECK IF A NUMBER IS PRIME

```java
public class PrimeCheck {
    public static void main(String[] args) {
        int num = 29;
        boolean isPrime = true;

        for (int i = 2; i <= num / 2; i++) {
            if (num % i == 0) {
                isPrime = false;
                break;
            }
        }

        if (isPrime) {
            System.out.println(num + " is a prime number.");
        } else {
```

```
            System.out.println(num + " is not a prime number.");
        }
    }
}
```

Output:

29 is a prime number.

249. FIND THE FIRST N PRIME NUMBERS

```java
public class FirstNPrimes {
    public static void main(String[] args) {
        int n = 10;
        int count = 0;
        int num = 2;

        while (count < n) {
            boolean isPrime = true;

            for (int i = 2; i <= Math.sqrt(num); i++) {
                if (num % i == 0) {
                    isPrime = false;
                    break;
                }
            }
```

```java
            if (isPrime) {
                System.out.print(num + " ");
                count++;
            }
            num++;
        }
    }
}
```

Output:

2 3 5 7 11 13 17 19 23 29

250. FIND THE NTH FIBONACCI NUMBER

```java
public class NthFibonacci {
    public static void main(String[] args) {
        int n = 10;
        int a = 0, b = 1, fib = 0;

        for (int i = 2; i <= n; i++) {
            fib = a + b;
            a = b;
            b = fib;
        }
        System.out.println("The " + n + "th Fibonacci number is: " + fib);
    }
}
```

Output:

The 10th Fibonacci number is: 34

251. CONVERT DECIMAL TO BINARY

```java
public class DecimalToBinary {
    public static void main(String[] args) {
        int num = 10;
        String binary = "";

        while (num > 0) {
            binary = (num % 2) + binary;
            num = num / 2;
        }
        System.out.println("Binary representation: " + binary);
    }
}
```

Output:

Binary representation: 1010

252. CONVERT BINARY TO DECIMAL

```java
public class BinaryToDecimal {
    public static void main(String[] args) {
        String binary = "1010";
        int decimal = 0;
        for (int i = 0; i < binary.length(); i++) {
            if (binary.charAt(i) == '1') {
                decimal += Math.pow(2, binary.length() - 1 - i);
            }
        }

        System.out.println("Decimal representation: " + decimal);
    }
}
```

Output:

Decimal representation: 10

253. FIND THE LARGEST ELEMENT IN A 2D ARRAY

```java
public class LargestElement2DArray {
    public static void main(String[] args) {
        int[][] array = {
            {1, 2, 3},
            {4, 5, 6},
            {7, 8, 9}
        };

        int max = array[0][0];

        for (int[] row : array) {
            for (int num : row) {
                if (num > max) {
                    max = num;
                }
            }
```

```
        }


    System.out.println("Largest element in the 2D array: " + max);
  }
}
```

Output:

Largest element in the 2D array: 9

254. CHECK IF A NUMBER IS ARMSTRONG

```java
public class ArmstrongCheck {
    public static void main(String[] args) {
        int num = 153;
        int originalNum = num;
        int result = 0;

        while (originalNum != 0) {
            int remainder = originalNum % 10;
            result += Math.pow(remainder, 3);
            originalNum /= 10;
        }

        if (result == num) {
            System.out.println(num + " is an Armstrong number.");
        } else {
```

```
            System.out.println(num + " is not an Armstrong number.");
        }
    }
}
```

Output:

153 is an Armstrong number.

255. FIND THE SUM OF DIGITS OF A NUMBER

```java
public class SumOfDigits {
    public static void main(String[] args) {
        int num = 12345;
        int sum = 0;

        while (num > 0) {
            sum += num % 10;
            num = num / 10;
        }

        System.out.println("Sum of digits: " + sum);
    }
}
```

Output:

Sum of digits: 15

256. REVERSE A NUMBER

```java
public class ReverseNumber {
    public static void main(String[] args) {
        int num = 12345;
        int reversed = 0;
        while (num != 0) {
            int digit = num % 10;
            reversed = reversed * 10 + digit;
            num /= 10;
        }
        System.out.println("Reversed number: " + reversed);
    }
}
```

Output:

Reversed number: 54321

257. CHECK IF A NUMBER IS PALINDROME

```java
public class PalindromeNumber {
    public static void main(String[] args) {
        int num = 121;
        int originalNum = num;
        int reversed = 0;

        while (num != 0) {
            int digit = num % 10;
            reversed = reversed * 10 + digit;
            num /= 10;
        }

        if (originalNum == reversed) {
            System.out.println(originalNum + " is a palindrome number.");
        } else {
```

```java
        System.out.println(originalNum + " is not a palindrome number.");
    }
  }
}
```

Output:

121 is a palindrome number.

258. FIND THE FREQUENCY OF EACH CHARACTER IN A STRING

```java
import java.util.HashMap;
import java.util.Map;

public class FrequencyOfCharacters {
    public static void main(String[] args) {
        String str = "hello world";
        Map<Character, Integer> charCountMap = new HashMap<>();

        for (char c : str.toCharArray()) {
            charCountMap.put(c, charCountMap.getOrDefault(c, 0) + 1);
        }

        for (Map.Entry<Character, Integer> entry : charCountMap.entrySet()) {
```

```
        System.out.println(entry.getKey() + ": " + entry.getValue());
    }
  }
}
```

Output:

```makefile
Copy code
h: 1
e: 1
l: 3
o: 2
 : 1
w: 1
r: 1
d: 1
```

www.ingramcontent.com/pod-product-compliance
Lightning Source LLC
Chambersburg PA
CBHW052138220526
45471CB00004B/1436